# CROWN PRINCE OF THE WHISKERINOS

## Zachary Taylor Wilcox and the Days of '49 Celebration, Sacramento, 1922

Carolyn Mirich

Grateful acknowledgement is made for both research and permission to reprint material from the following: Sacramento Archives & Museum Collection Center, with special thanks to Dylan McDonald, CA, Archivist; Meade Simpson; the *Sacramento Bee*; the *Nevada Appeal*; the University of Nevada Reno; Stanford University Libraries; the National Museum of Natural History; Sacramento Public Library, Sacramento Room, with special thanks to Tom Tolley; Nevada Historical Society; Nevada State Library and Archives; Lone Mountain Cemetery; the Sons of Union Veterans of the Civil War; the National Archives and Records Administration; and to all who supplied photos and information. Very special thanks to Brittany Ferry, Liz McKinnell, and Hayley Mirich for help with all the details. Cover photo printed with permission from the *Sacramento Bee*.

A special thank you to Elinor Berger, who hooked and reeled me into the intriguing world of archive mining, and Laurien E. Riehl, great-grand-nephew of Zachary Wilcox, who first told me of his uncle with the long beard, leading me to this story and its mysterious loose end. Special thanks to Larry Nicodemus, great-great-grand-nephew of Zachary Taylor Wilcox, who has provided information from his collection.

To all who have attempted to solve this very whiskery mystery, thank you.

### Author's Notes

Names, places, incidents and whiskers referred to in this book are not based on the author's imagination. This story has been reconstructed using information from various archives, newspapers, libraries, and other sources with assumed credibility. Acknowledgement is made that the Days of '49 Celebration was the result of the planning and participation of numerous volunteers, clubs, and organizations throughout the city of Sacramento. The focus here is on the Whiskerinos with no intention of slighting other groups and their contributions.

Copyright © 2006 Carolyn Mirich

All rights reserved, including the right of reproduction in whole or
in part in any form.

ISBN: 1-4196-3086-5

Library of Congress Control Number: 2006901955

Publisher: BookSurge, LLC
5341 Dorchester Rd., Suite 16
North Charleston, SC 29418
www.booksurge.com
1-866-308-6235

# Dedication

To the spirit of the pioneers of the Golden West,

Whiskerinos and Whiskerettes everywhere.

*I give to my subjects, and all members of the Whiskers Club of Camp '49 and all loyal Whiskerinos, in trust for their children, all and every, the flowers of the field and the blossoms of the woods, with the right to play among them freely according to the customs of '49, warning them at the same time against thistles and thorns; and I devise to my subjects the banks of the brooks of the region of '49 and the golden sands beneath the waters thereof, and the odors of the willows that dip therein, and the white clouds that float high over the largest trees in the world, which grow near Camp '49, and I leave the children of my subjects the long, long days to be merry in, in a thousand ways, and the night and the moon and the train of the Milky Way to wonder at, but subject nevertheless to the rights hereinafter given to lovers of the Golden West.*

—Zachary Taylor Wilcox, Last Will and Testament

# Table of Contents

| | | |
|---|---|---|
| Whiskery Words | | 6 |
| Chapter One | Fateful Words | 7 |
| Chapter Two | Pre-Fame Farming | 9 |
| Chapter Three | Call of the West | 15 |
| Chapter Four | Event of an Era | 17 |
| Chapter Five | The Whiskerinos of Sacramento | 33 |
| Chapter Six | Days of '49 Celebration | 43 |
| Chapter Seven | A Higher Calling | 53 |
| Chapter Eight | Zack's Final Lessons to His Subjects | 55 |
| Chapter Nine | The Last Word | 57 |
| Chapter Ten | "A Few Days Anyway" and Some 80 Years Later | 61 |
| Chapter Eleven | The Final Stop | 63 |
| Epilogue | | 67 |
| Whiskers Alive | | 71 |
| Days of '49 Memorabilia | | 73 |
| Appendix | | 83 |
| Bibliography | | 101 |
| Index | | 103 |

# *Whiskery Words*

**For those unfamiliar with the world of whiskers:**

**adornment**

>*The act of decorating yourself with something colorful and interesting, even something shaggy and bristly.*

**bewhiskered/biwhiskered**

>*Having hair on the cheeks and chin; bearded, barbate, whiskered, whiskery.*

**crown prince**

>*Male heir/hair apparent to the throne.*

**hirsute** \HUR-soot; HIR-soot; hur-SOOT; hir-SOOT\,

>*Covered with hair; set with bristles; shaggy; hairy.*

**Whiskerette**

>*Small bit of hair on the chin, or a woman, with or without facial bristles, who was a member of the Whiskerette Club of Camp '49.*

**Whiskerino**

>*Beard-growing contest participant or a gentleman who was a member of the Days of '49 Whisker Club.*

**Whiskerite**

>*Whisker wearer not crowned King or Crown Prince during the Days of '49.*

## Chapter One
## **Fateful Words**

The following story has come to light after years of incessant pleading, coaxing, and downright begging for information from newspapers, historical societies, museums, universities, the U.S. Government, the states of California and Nevada, libraries, cemeteries, and relatives of Zachary Wilcox. What began with one photo and hearsay information about an old gentleman with a long beard born 160 years ago has blossomed into a story of the undying spirit of the pioneers that made this great country and those who celebrate them. It is the story of a simple farmer who grew up to become a Crown Prince, ***and all that implies.***

The mysterious end of the story may be a good place to start in this tale of whiskery wonder. There was a very real, truly legal, and very bewhiskered will. The fateful words to transfer custody of the whiskers were signed by Zachary Taylor Wilcox, at the age of 76. The will, which was legally signed and witnessed, was prepared by Arthur H. McCurdy, attorney and fellow Whiskerino, of Sacramento, California.

Nearly 80 years after Zachary's death, there is still a cloud of mystery that lingers. To this day, only part of Zack can be accounted for.

He wasn't always in possession of something worthy of intense interest and which would ultimately lead him to becoming a Crown Prince. Before all the pomp and circumstance, he was a simple farmer in Vermont.

Zachary Taylor Wilcox. Courtesy of Larry Nicodemus

## Chapter Two
## Pre-Fame Farming

The tale still unraveling began on a farm in Whitingham, Vermont, nearly 160 years ago. On April 2, 1847, Zachary Taylor Wilcox entered the world of his parents, Andrew and Sarah (Parsons) Wilcox. He had two older sisters, Sally and Fiducia, but the male influence ruled the Wilcox household. Zack had just become the sixth brother, joining Andrew, John, Silas, Charles Luman, and George. Being the youngest, with so many brothers, provided the necessary training for his future endeavors in mostly fraternal organizations.

Zack was fourteen years old at the outbreak of the Civil War and working on a farm with his brothers. His brother Charles Luman had enlisted in September 1862, but died of disease shortly thereafter on December 29, 1862, at the age of 22. He died in Alexandria, Virginia. It is not known whether Silas served. During the last year of the conflict, selectmen came to town to fill quotas for the army. John Wilcox enlisted in the 1st Vermont Cavalry Company F. Zachary was only eighteen but determined to become a soldier. Since he was underage, Zack found that he would need parental consent to enlist. His father Andrew accompanied young Zack to the recruiter, gave his consent, his signature, and his blessing. Zachary was mustered in as a private in the 1st Vermont Cavalry Company F on September 22, 1864, joining his brother John. Zack's brother George also enlisted that year but entered the 31st Massachusetts Regiment. Brother Andrew tried to enlist but did not pass muster. Though he stayed home, his heart remained with his brothers. So it came to be that the brothers Wilcox found themselves in the middle of the Civil War.

The 1st Vermont Cavalry was involved in many battles, including Sheridan's raid, Waynesboro, the Battle of Cedar Creek, the occupation of Charlottesville, and the Appomattox campaign, where Lee surrendered to Grant. Zachary and John served under General George Armstrong Custer in the 2nd Brigade, 3rd Division. On November 2, 1864, John was wounded at the Battle of Cedar Creek. His official hospital papers state that he was thrown by a horse. George served in the mounted infantry until the end of the war. He was a marksman of renown with a rifle.

Zachary was discharged June 21, 1865, with distinguished service. When he was mustered out, Zack said he wished to retain one Remington Revolver, a belt, and Spencer Carbine. For these he was charged $33.33. After the war, Zack and his brother George served in the Grand Army of the Republic (G.A.R.). They remained active members of G.A.R. Custer Corps No. 15 in Carson City, serving their country until the end of their days.

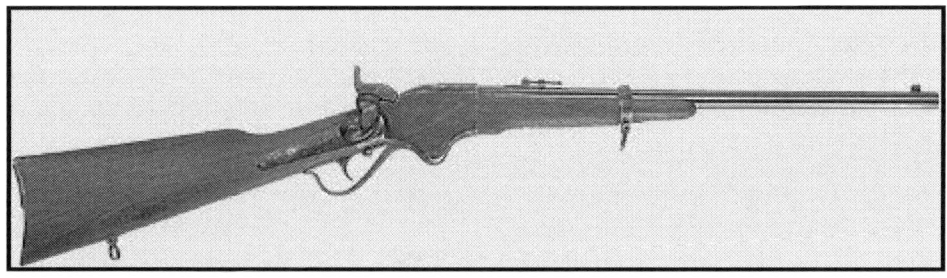

Spencer Carbine

| | 1 Cav. | Vt. |

Zachary T. Wilcox
Pvt. , Co. F , 1 Reg't Vermont Cavalry.
Age 18 years.
Appears on a
**Detachment Muster-out Roll**
of the organization named above. Roll dated
Burlington, Vt., June 21, 1865.
Muster-out to date June 21, 1865.
Last paid to Dec. 31, 1864.
Clothing account:
Last settled Nov. , 186 ; drawn since $37 41/100
Due soldier $ 100/100; due U. S. $ 100/100
Am't for cloth'g in kind or money adv'd $ 100/100
Due U. S. for arms, equipments, &c., $ 100/100
Bounty paid $33 33/100; due $93 33/100
Valuation of horse, $ 100/100
Valuation of horse equipments, $ 100/100
Remarks: Wishes to retain one Remington Revolver, Belt and Carbine Spencer.
Book mark :

(449) Grogan, Copyist.

---

| | 1 Cav. | Vt. |

Zackery T. Wilcox
Pvt. , New Co. , 1 Reg't Vermont Cav.
Age 18 years.
Appears on **Co. Muster-out Roll**, dated
Burlington Vt. Aug. 9, 1865.
Muster-out to date , 186 .
Last paid to , 186 .
Clothing account:
Last settled , 186 ; drawn since $ 100/100
Due soldier $ 100/100; due U. S. $ 100/100
Am't for cloth'g in kind or money adv'd $ 100/100
Due U. S. for arms, equipments, &c., $ 100/100
Bounty paid $ 100/100; due $ 100/100
Valuation of horse, $ 100/100
Valuation of horse equipments, $ 100/100
Remarks: Discharged from F Comp'y. Disch'g'd Pr. G. O. No. 83 W. D. A. G. O. June 20. 1865.

Book mark :

(361) Copyist.

Zachary Taylor Wilcox in his G.A.R. uniform.
Private Collection. Reprinted by permission from Larry Nicodemus.

## Grand Army of the Republic, Custer Corps No. 15, Carson City, Nevada

Top Row, Left to Right: J. Beckstead (Mexican American War), George Meyers, Horace F. Bartine, George Wilcox, Zachary Wilcox. Seated Left to Right: John McCullough, Jason C. Burlingame, Governor D. S. Dickerson (Spanish American War), C. A. Braslin (sic). Photo taken May 30, 1910. Private Collection. Reprinted by permission from Laurien E. Riehl.

*Go West, young man,*

*and grow up with the country.*

—Horace Greeley

## Chapter Three

## Call of the West

Following his Civil War service, Zack may have returned home to work on the farm temporarily, but his path soon took another direction—west. The largest migration of people in American history was underway. Thousands were heading west on a quest for adventure, gold, or a better life. Towns were sprouting up all along the foothills of the Sierra Nevadas. Zack's brother Andrew had already made the journey with his wife Eliza (descendant of Revolutionary War patriot Roger Amidon) and their children. They settled in Forest Ranch, near Chico, California. In 1876 George and his wife Ella also went to California.

Andrew Asahel Wilcox and George Almon Wilcox. Private Collection.
Reprinted by permission from Larry Nicodemus.

It seemed only natural that Zack would find his way west as well. With dreams of gold and the need for adventure, he took a slightly different route. Zack was one of the early pioneers of the Alaska Gold Rush. He tried his luck with prospecting and some said that might be where the beard may have begun to serve a purpose—protecting his chest from the Yukon cold. Another theory was that he lost an election bet and yet another was that he cut himself shaving with a dull razor and swore never to shave again. Whatever the story or the reason, the seed was planted and the nurturing began on the road that would lead to fame and royalty.

When Zack was thirty years old, he joined Andrew and George near Chico to try his hand at mining. The three brothers were together again. Not laden with gold, Zack and George's family made their way to Carson City. George found work as a carpenter and, along with his wife Ella, raised three children. Andrew, after the death of his wife Eliza in 1885 and his remarriage to Ruth Handy, also moved to Carson City. Why Carson City? We may never know, but whatever the reason, Carson City was where the three Wilcox brothers put down roots.

Zack continued to do a great deal of prospecting but the practical Zack purchased a home and spent his days doing concrete work. He made a comfortable living, supplemented by his Civil War pension of $72 per month. The brick and concrete laid by Zack throughout Carson City undoubtedly still contain tiny thread-like outgrowths which fell from the now famous whiskers.

## Chapter Four
## **Event of an Era**

Zack continued his work in Carson City and cultivated his chin crop until people began to take notice. He was often followed by curious children who asked to see his long beard. Who would have thought that a few whiskers could create such a stir? Who would have guessed that because of his facial growth, Zack would gain the attention of a city 150 miles away and soon find himself hobnobbing with everyone who was anyone in Sacramento during the Days of '49 Celebration?

The 1920s were a very exciting time in the growing city of Sacramento. The worst was behind—the war had ended, as had the flu epidemic of 1918–1919, which infected thousands of Sacramentans and killed 500. Women now had the right to vote. Sacramento was enjoying the good times of the roaring twenties, complete with speakeasies and flappers. The only damper put on the fun might have been Prohibition.

According to city historian James Henley, "Sacramento in the '20s was like Sacramento in the 1850s. It was a hot, alive, lustful town. And the city also came upon the sense of its past in terms of romance. That's not so new to the '20s, but the '20s took it to a high point. They began to look at the past and turned it into a romanticized version of history: The miner is heroic. Great men achieved great things. Labor was hard but heroic." This period came as a great respite after the pain of war and illness.

As early as 1920 planning was underway in Sacramento for the Days of '49 Celebration to be held in 1922. The year 1920 was also the year the voters of Sacramento adopted their City Charter (municipal constitution) and a City Council/City Manager form of government, still used today. The city also had in place organized lobbying to be sure the federal government didn't forget Sacramento, and city fathers were pushing for a port and more military bases. Sacramento had a finely tuned Chamber of Commerce and civic leaders who ably pulled off a brilliant publicity campaign. According to Meade Simpson, the original idea for the Days of '49 Celebration came from his father, Edgar Simpson (rancher), Bill Elliott (Star Auto), and Cliff Russell (prominent attorney). They convinced corporations and civic leaders to hold the celebration. There were estimates that this gala attracted 100,000 visitors from across the country and around the world. The unprecedented success of the Days of '49 Celebration was the result of city leaders who were able to inspire the involvement of nearly every citizen of Sacramento. The event celebrated the founding of the city in 1849 and the beginning of the gold rush the same year. The city's leaders hoped that this event would create an interest and draw tourists to Sacramento well into the future.

The publicity blitz to promote this huge event began with the printing of over 200,000 leaflets. The dates were set for May 23–28, 1922. Historical booklets were printed by the Chamber titled "The Romance of California." (See page 75.)

Publicity reached every corner of the nation. All news media members were given free passes to the event. The Chamber distributed over 5,000 dress patterns to citizens of Sacramento to sew costumes. Merchants made wood planks which covered the sidewalks. An official souvenir song, "Days of '49," was even composed for the occasion, words by George S. Tyner and set to music by Maurice Silverman. (See page 79.)

Bill Elliott was in charge of the parades and the rodeo. Edgar Simpson was the arena director and he personally put up $3,500.00 for the event, which was a great deal of money in 1922.

Lapel buttons were distributed to Sacramentans by the thousands to be worn until the end of the celebration. Citizen involvement was crucial to its success. Over 1,000 people were involved in the planning of spectacular events which would last throughout the Days of '49 Celebration, revealing a sense of community and civic awareness not often associated with the "Wild West." With so many visitors expected in Sacramento, the city leaders put out a call to all citizens to house visitors and rent out rooms. At the time, the city of Sacramento had a population of 65,908. Another 100,000 in visitors would definitely have put a strain on city resources without the cooperation of all the citizens.

Plans were made for the construction of a mining town at the Southern Pacific yard, and relics of pioneer days started arriving from across the country for the displays. C. A. "Ab" Ambrose shipped three carloads of artifacts from San Francisco, which included a hand fire engine used in San Francisco in 1850. A fifty-year-old carriage came from Carson City's Benton's Stable, where Hank Monk started his famous drive with Horace Greeley. Also on exhibit were a Concord stagecoach and a sword used in the Mexican War. Carson City joined the festivities, sending mining trophies for display. A cannon arrived from Volcano, California.

Groups made plans to attend from across the country. From the Carson City and Reno area, over 100 members of the Washoe and Piute tribes made plans to attend with their families. An Indian camp was incorporated into the Mining Town.

Fun was the credo in Sacramento, as the community planned for the big event. Back in Carson City, however, Zack went about life as usual.

By 1915 Zack's beard had reached eight and a half feet in length, substantially longer than his 5'5" stature. Leaving it to the mercy of the winds and weather might have caused considerable logistical problems for a man who worked as a stonecutter and mason. Augustus Dougherty, whose article on Zack was in the Nevada State Museum files, said, "This remarkable beard, though quite heavy, was very silky in texture." He described Zack as a very modest man who "carried the beard in his bosom where it was always concealed from public view, a method he practiced through life." Dougherty said Zack declined "flattering offers to appear in museums and publicly exhibit his wonderful beard." Zack was known to wrap his beard around a piece of cardboard and place it securely in his vest. A much shorter outer beard was all that was shown in public.

Zachary Wilcox. Private Collection. Reprinted by permission from Larry Nicodemus and Elinor Berger.

Even without his wonderful beard, Zack had become a very well recognized man about town. Zack had other interests outside mining and watching his whiskers grow. For more than twenty years Zack had ridden around Carson City on a high-wheeled bicycle. This was yet another good reason to keep his hirsute adornment under wrap. He continued riding even after he had written and signed his whisker will.

His was a bicycle with a seat about five feet off the ground. The high-wheeled bicycle has a reputation of being one of the most dangerous bicycles ever built. Riders were often pitched over the front wheel onto their heads. Mark Twain said after riding one, "Get a bicycle. You will not regret it if you live." The high-wheeled bicycles had unreliable braking systems where riders had to pedal backwards to slow to a stop. While riding downhill, riders often put their feet up on the handlebars in order to jump off quickly in case of emergency. Riding such a bicycle might likely have been considered an extreme sport of the day. The riders defying gravity at such a height would likely either have been of sturdy pioneer stock or perhaps just bent on self-destruction.

Zachary had become a familiar sight in Carson City as he rode with a parrot by the name of Polly on the handlebars. They were of great interest to local children and the talk of the town. While riding his bicycle one day, Zack tried to avoid being hit by one car and was struck by another. Turning on a dime was not easily done on a high-wheeled bicycle. It was said that perhaps his amazing beard provided a certain amount of protection during the fall. He fractured his leg but made a remarkable recovery. After his accident, however, he vowed not to take Polly for rides on the bicycle any longer, fearing not for himself, but that he may fall and injure her.

As Zack continued growing his whiskers and riding high, the citizens of Sacramento remained busy rekindling the spirit of the 1850s. Since early pioneers and miners, like Zack, often sported a variety of whiskers, the Whiskers Club of Camp '49 was founded to add excitement and color to the Days of '49 Celebration. Much of this event was planned by members of the Whiskers Club, which included Clyde L. Seavey, the first City Manager of Sacramento and Chief Whiskerino; H. E. Diggles, Vice Whiskerino; Arthur Dudley, Chamber of Commerce Manager; and Irvin Engler, Assistant Chamber Manager. Other prominent Whiskerinos were Judge Elijah C. Hart, of the Third District Court of Appeals; Harry Peterson, Custodian of the Museum at Sutter's Fort; and Arthur H. McCurdy, attorney. Membership of the Whiskerinos eventually numbered in the thousands. The Whiskerinos held huge meetings under a variety of hats in the basement of the Chamber of Commerce Building on 7th Street.

Whiskerinos Meeting, Basement of the Chamber of Commerce, ca. 1922, 1980/04/01, Arthur H. McCurdy Collection, Sacramento Archives & Museum Collection Center.

May 19, 1922, marked the day the Articles of Incorporation were filed with the Secretary of State of the State of California for the "Whiskers Club of Camp '49." Two years later, Articles of Incorporation were also filed for the "Whiskerette Club of Camp '49." (See Appendix.)

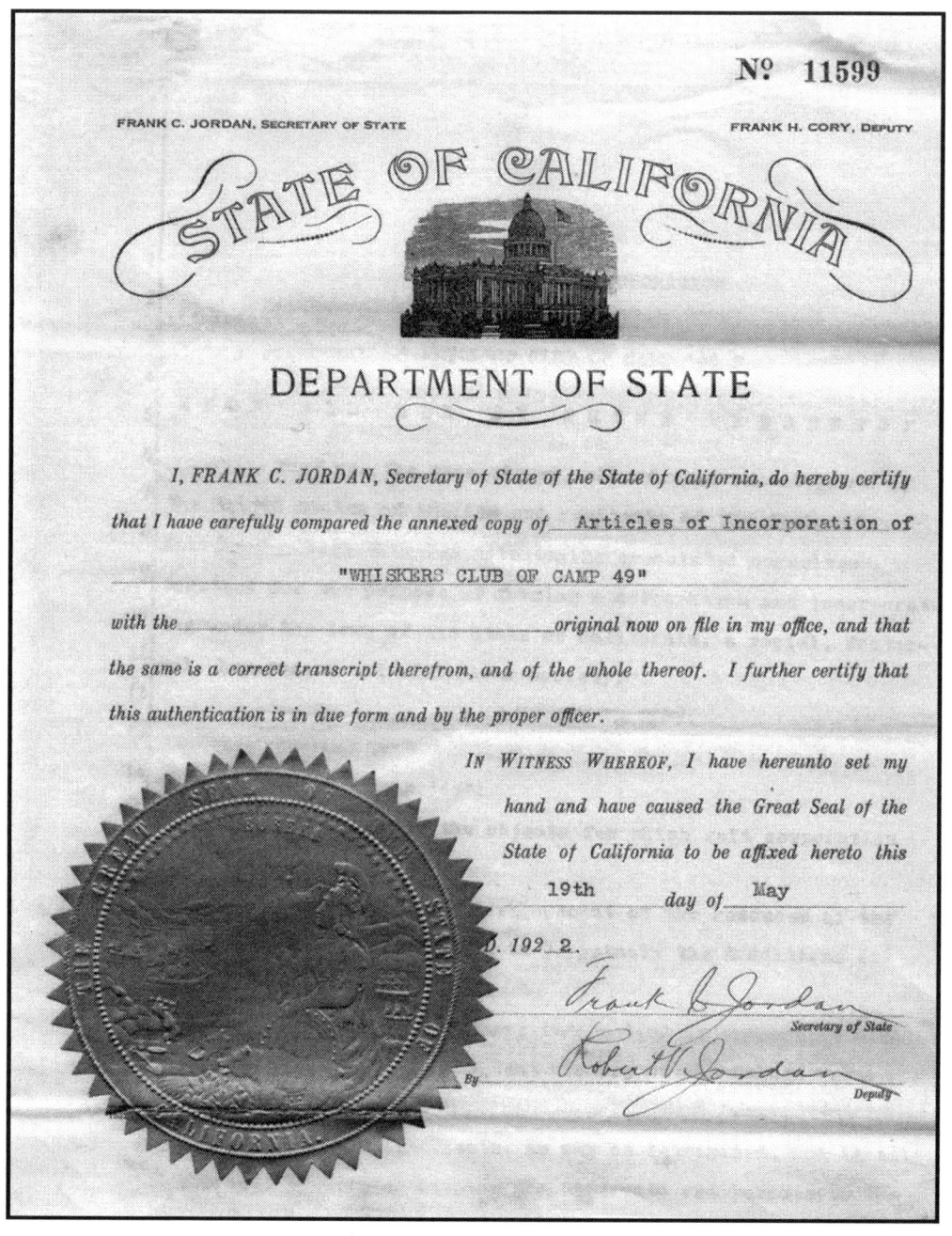

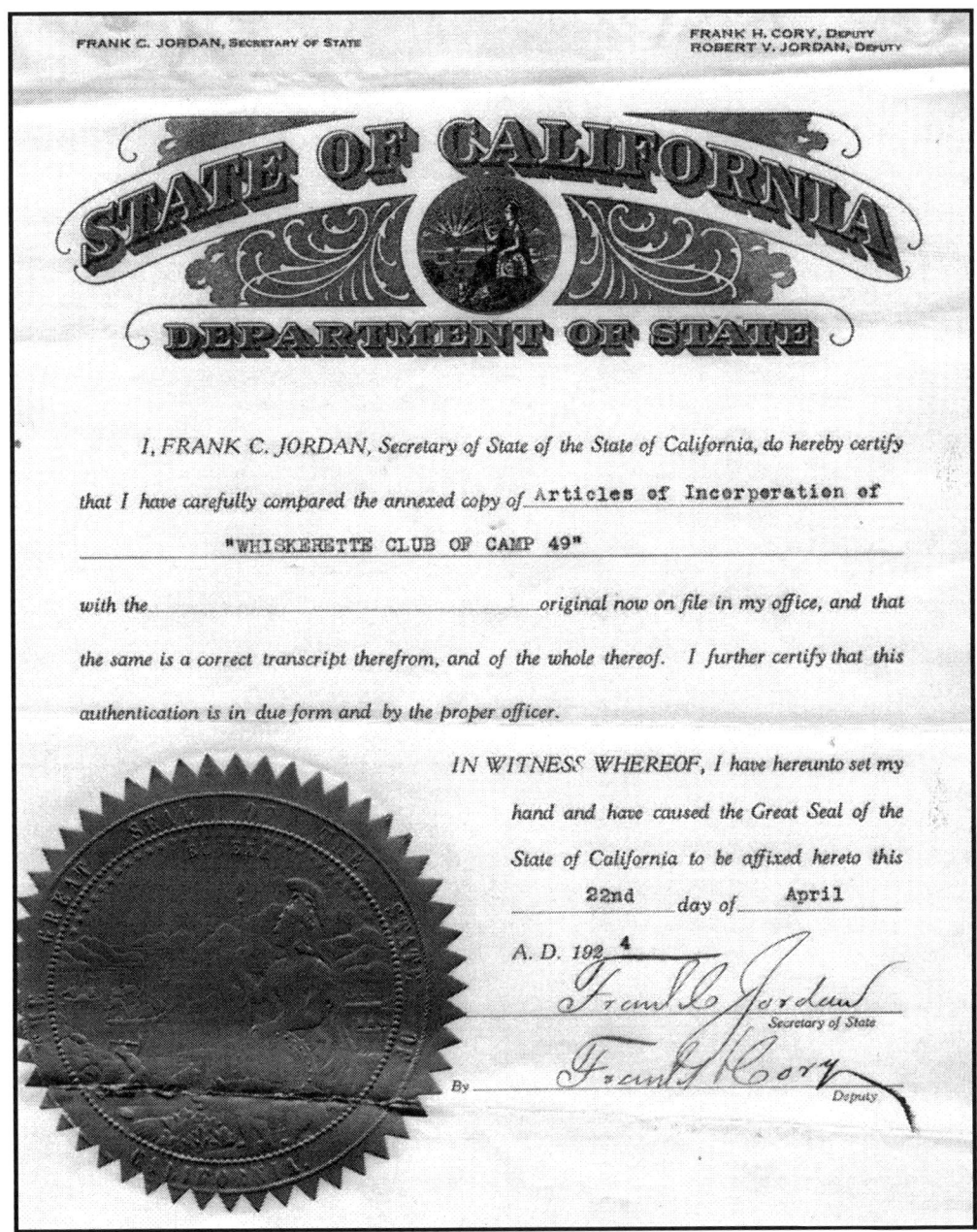

Articles of Incorporation Files, Sacramento County Clerk Collection. Sacramento Archives & Museum Collection Center.

Letters were sent out to Whiskerinos for meetings at places such as McKinney's at Lake Tahoe (now Chambers). One mass mailing stated there was to be a bear hunt at McKinney's, also known as the "Hangout of the Whiskerinos". Committees were appointed to locate bear pits and caves and to hold a preliminary bear hunt. The presumed purpose of the meetings was to plan the festivities for the Days of '49.

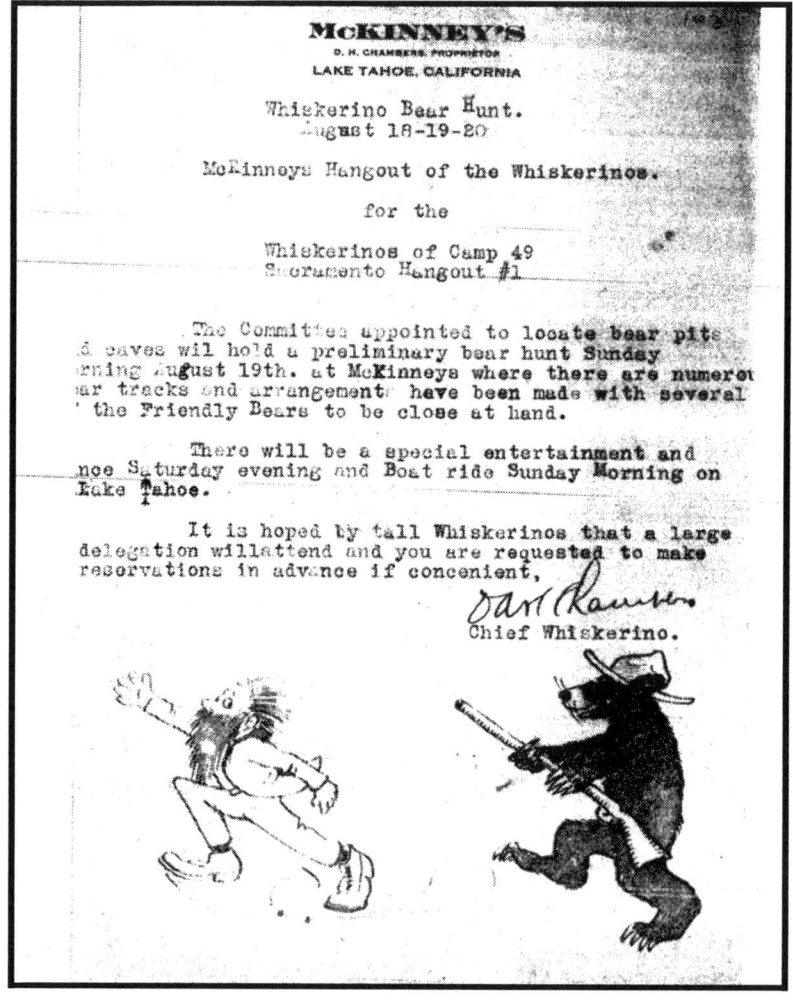

Harry C. Peterson Papers, ca. 1880–1994, M0649, Courtesy of Department of Special Collections. Reprinted by permission from Stanford University Libraries.

The Dress of the Days of '49, Reich & Lievre Girls, Sacramento Store. Reprinted by permission from Sacramento Room, Sacramento Public Library.

With the March 2, 1922, *Sacramento Bee* headline, "Whiskers to be '49 Days Password," publicity for the whisker contest kicked into high gear. The nationwide search was on for the longest beard. The man with the longest beard in the United States would be the recipient of a roundtrip fare to Sacramento, an engraved gold medal in commemoration of the event, and would reign over all other whiskerites.

On March 7, 1922, J. L. LaRash, Chairman of the Whiskers Committee, announced to the Chamber of Commerce Ad Club the rules for the Days of '49 whisker contest. These rules were:

1. Contestants had to be clean-shaven on St. Patrick's Day, March 17, 1922. Every contestant had to submit a certificate signed by a Sacramento barber that he was shaven on March 17, the opening day of the contest. Contestants would be handed membership cards and handsome buttons designating the wearer as a member of the Whisker Club.

Membership Card. Private Collection. Printed by permission of Meade Simpson.

2. Hair tonics could be used as desired.

3. First prize for the longest beard grown between March 17 and the end of the Days of '49 Celebration would be a cash prize of $49.

4. Merchandise prizes would be given to winners of categories which included neatness of appearance, longest mustache, best looking whiskers, most brilliantly colored whiskers, best imitation of sagebrush, length, luxuriance of growth, etc.

5. Contestants were to line up at the Mining Town on the second day of the celebration to be inspected by the judges. The three judges were the President of the Barber's Union, Mrs. Helen Gilmore, President of the Women's Council, and Clyde Seavey."

With the rules laid out, the fun began!

Clyde Seavey, City Manager and Chief Whiskerino, sent a letter to King George V, making him an honorary member of the Whiskers Club. Other letters were sent to the Secretary of State, Charles Evans Hughes, former Senator J. H. Lewis, Senator Henry Cabot Lodge, and other famous whisker growers.

Letter to King George:

> To His most Gracious Majesty King George the Fifth
>
> Will his Majesty deign to grant the distinguished honor of conferring his patronage upon the Whiskers Club of Sacramento, California, and the worthy purpose for which it is organized?

To revive the memorable events of the great Gold Rush to California, the City of Sacramento is extending to the world an invitation to join with it from May 23 to 28 in the 'Days of '49' celebration. Its citizens will revive the pleasures and pastimes of that period and its men will wear the whiskers emblematic of the hardy and determined pioneers.

May it please His Majesty to know that his own gracious adoption and cultivation of whiskers has commanded the admiration of the members of the Whisker Club and that his Majesty's example is now the worthy guide for the ambition of its members.

In appreciation of this fact, the Whiskers Club is moved to present his Majesty this humble request that he accept the patronage of its activities and is respectfully informed that he has been made an Honorary Member of the club.

THE WHISKERS CLUB OF SACRAMENTO

Mr. Clyde L. Seavey

Chief Whiskerino

Membership card sent to King George. *Sacramento Bee*, May 4, 1922.

With hundreds of onlookers and "flanked by pretty girls and women garbed in the styles of '49," the *Sacramento Bee* reported on March 17, 1922, charter members of the club were publicly shaved in front of the Post Office while cameras clicked and motion picture machines were put to work. Several policemen were needed to hold back the crowd to make room for "tonsorial artists" to demonstrate their skills. The stage was set on the street with old-style barber chairs and buckets of hot water on soap boxes. J. L. LaRash sounded a gong starting the scraping process. First in the very uncomfortable chairs were General Chairman H. E. Diggles, City Manager Clyde Seavey, W. L. Swannell, G. M. Templeton, M. D. Smith, E. P. Smith and D. G. Nunneley. Thirty women and girls, headed by Mrs. Frank Bellhouse, pinned badges on all the entrants as they left the chairs. William Graham, who said he was a "real forty-niner," had five-inch whiskers removed to start the contest. It took two barbers to shave him as the crowd cheered on. It was estimated that news photos of this public shaving would be seen by fifty million people throughout the world. Cameramen from the Selbnick News, the Kinograms, the Pathe News, and the International were on hand taking pictures of this most unusual contest.

1981/01/1332, Sacramento Photography Survey Collection, Sacramento Archives & Museum Collection Center.

On April 4, 1922, the first grand mobilization of the Whisker Club took place. One hundred seats were reserved in the grandstand at Moreing Park for the opening day of baseball season. The seats were directly behind third base and members of the club were invited to make a public showing of their hair-growing progress. The new ballpark had an estimated 13,500 in attendance on opening day. Gov. William Stephens threw out the first pitch to City Manager and Chief Whiskerino Clyde Seavey. A special train was also secured to take the '49 Whisker Club to San Francisco to make an appearance at ball games at the Pacific Coast League grounds.

Members of the Whisker Club kept a high profile around town in the days leading up to the Days of '49. They attended ball games, participated in parades and were filmed by moviemakers. Five motion picture companies filmed approximately 3,000 Whiskerinos in costume at the State Capitol. The Whiskerinos were reviewed by Governor Stephens. The films were released across the nation.

Word had circulated about Zack's amazing beard and Zack was paid a visit by Arthur Dudley, Manager of the Sacramento Chamber of Commerce. According to the *Sacramento Bee*, April 15, 1922, after traveling to Carson City and meeting with Zack, Dudley stated that he had "used a periscope to see Wilcox behind the brush." Zack was invited to the event and told he would occupy a hut at the '49 Camp, where he would play the part of a hermit. Arrangements went forward for Zack to exhibit his beard at the celebration. It was believed he had the world's longest beard.

## Chapter Five

## The Whiskerinos of Sacramento

The Whiskerinos considered a smooth face a high crime to be put before a Whiskerino jury. The Whiskerinos' jury also issued warrants for treason, which were served by the sheriff of the Whiskerinos.

Headlines on Wednesday, May 10, 1922, in the *Sacramento Bee* read:

**WHISKERS COURT ENFORCES GROWTH,**

**Citizens Are Ordered to Do Their Civic Duty; Many Are Sentenced.**

> Before a crowd of red-shirted Whiskerinos and their women friends which filled the main floor of the Chamber of Commerce and overflowed into the lobby and upon the mezzanine floor, the Kangaroo Court of the Whisker Club last night continued its uproarious way, collecting fines from citizens who have failed in their civic duty of growing whiskers, and administering good-natured rebukes to others who are not giving the Days of '49 wholehearted support.
>
> **Mysterious Stunt**
>
> Last night's session attracted a larger crowd than any previous meeting. Everybody stayed until some twenty-four cases had been disposed of when the Southern Pacific Glee Club was brought in under arrest and, after entertaining with several selections, its fines were remitted and the Court adjourned until Friday evening….
>
> **Sentenced to Make Trip**
>
> A number of the defendants before the Court last night were sentenced to make the trip to Chico Saturday with the club. Oroville and Marysville will be visited.
>
> Adjutant General J. J. Borres was among those hauled before the Court last night. He urged in his defense orders to a former Adjutant General of the State signed by President Taylor in which a smooth face was made mandatory by army regulations. He was found guilty.
>
> Robert Dundas of the Police Department was the center of a prolonged investigation and many witnesses were called; one of whom declared Dundas was the 'Grand Gobbler' of the 'three coo coos.' Dundas was charged with making false charges against members of the Kangaroo Court. He was found guilty and sentenced to go to Chico Saturday in the regalia of the K.K.K.

**Two More Guilty**

Charles Bliss was hailed before the Court on charges of 'claiming to be a City Commissioner when the office was extinct.' He was fined $5 for his lack of beard. Another victim of the evening was Fontaine Johnson, described as 'one of those seeking to purify the county government.' Like the others, he was guilty as charged.

Jeff LaRash of the *Sacramento Star* was sentenced to buy a feed for the *Star* newsboys before the next meeting of the Court, or be tried on charges of sedition.

Many others were fined before the court ended its session, bringing the total fines to $70.00. The money was to be used for publicity work by the Whisker Club.

The Whisker Club was determined that the participation in this event would be citywide. H. E. Diggles, General Chairman of the Days of '49, made a declaration in the *Sacramento Bee* on April 19, 1922, that "Sacramento men have got to get busy growing whiskers or this city will be charged with getting visitors under false pretenses." City Manager Clyde Seavey issued a formal notice to all employees of the city, including policemen and firemen, that he expected them to grow beards. Companies and clubs in the city were encouraged to offer prizes as incentives for their employees and members to join in this movement.

Whiskerinos at Sacramento Junior College, 1983/232/13235, Michael Benning Collection, Sacramento Archives & Museum Collection Center.

Throughout the United States and Canada, stories ran which declared that "Sacramento will be a city of bearded men during the celebration. The club issued an appeal to the men of Sacramento to make good as a civic duty, and another appeal to the women to lay aside their prejudices against whiskers for a few weeks in the interests of advertising Sacramento." (April 19, 1922, *Sacramento Bee.*)

Whiskerettes presenting the key to the city to the International President of the Mining Convention on the steps of the Senator Hotel. Adellia McCurdy McCabe is presenting the key. 1980/04/12, Arthur H. McCurdy Collection, Sacramento Archives & Museum Collection Center.

Pennant from Days of '49. Reprinted by permission from Sacramento Room, Sacramento Public Library.

Whiskerinos and Whiskerettes

Days of '49 Parade. Driver is Irv Engler. Behind is Dick Nunneley. Ca. 1922. 1980/04/21, Arthur H. McCurdy Collection, Sacramento Archives & Museum Collection Center.

Miner's Congress Parade, Sept. 29, 1924, Frank Galligher, Driver, Adellia McCurdy McCabe on right of seat. 1980/04/56, Arthur H. McCurdy Collection, Sacramento Archives & Museum Collection Center.

Whiskerettes' Club members dressed in costumes for Days of '49 Celebration. Ca. 1922. Top Row, Left to Right: Nona Archer, Mrs. Martha Archer. Front Row, Left to Right: Edith McCurdy, Adellia McCurdy McCabe, Mrs. Van Sandt, Mrs. Lillian Snider, Unknown. 1980/04/06, Arthur H. McCurdy Collection, Sacramento Archives & Museum Collection Center.

Whiskerino and Whiskerette Club members in front of The First Congregational Church of Sacramento. Ca. 1922. 1980/04/08 Arthur H. McCurdy Collection, Sacramento Archives & Museum Collection Center.

Women played another role in the Days of '49 with the formation of a Women's Secret Service System. Ten prominent local clubwomen were appointed to oversee the conduct of the '49 camp and dance hall. Mrs. Adams, a member of the Women's Vigilance Committee, would not divulge the identities of the women, but "promised that the camp and dance hall will be kept as clean as possible." The Women's Vigilance Committee was formed with the purpose of supervising the conduct of girls employed in the dance hall. The committee objected to the publicity that the dance hall was going to be "wide open". "Everyone in Oakland and San Francisco is talking of coming to Sacramento for the '49 Celebration with the object of seeing a 'wide open town.'" The Women's Secret Service System was instructed to work as quietly as possible and be inconspicuous in the crowds, but with absolute authority to enforce the law.

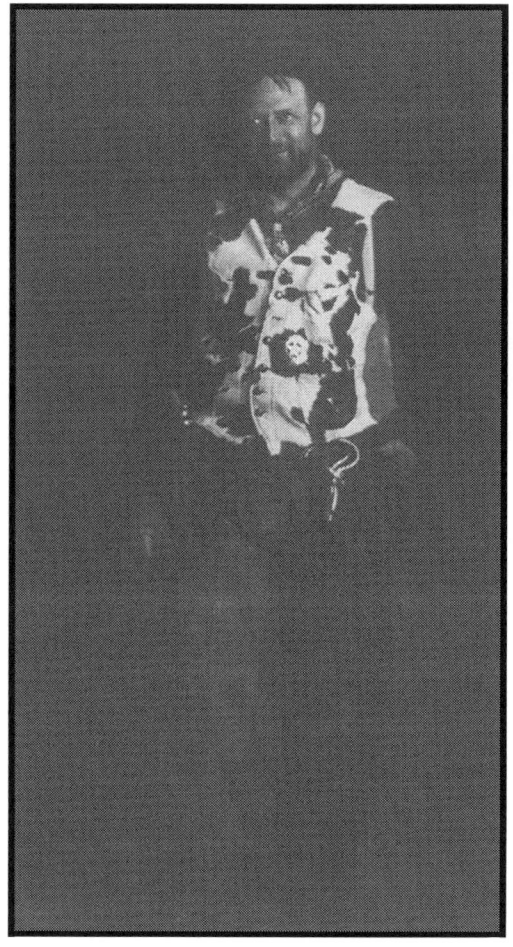

Sheriff Jos. Herspring, high Lord, Sheriff of the Whiskerinos, ca. 1922. 1980/04/05, Arthur H. McCurdy Collection, Sacramento Archives & Museum Collection Center.

Zachary Wilcox. Reprinted by permission from Nevada Historical Society, Carson City, Nevada.

Zachary Wilcox and his brother John Faxon Wilcox. Private Collection. Reprinted by permission from Larry Nicodemus.

## Chapter Six
## Days of '49 Celebration

As the days for the celebration in Sacramento drew nearer, it became unclear whether Zack, who had been ill, would be able to attend the celebration and participate in the contest. Luckily he recovered in time. After all, his beard couldn't attend without him. The beard Zack would accompany to Sacramento had last been brushed and groomed just nine years earlier when Zack had planned a trip to Vermont to visit relatives. At that time, the beard lost about two feet in length during the combing and trimming process. Since that time his beard had grown to a length of fourteen feet. It is assumed the beard was groomed again prior to the Days of '49 event. Zack felt that if he had given proper care to his beard, it could have grown to a length of twenty feet.

It was noted that the parade of the Whiskerinos "resembled the triumphant entry of a victorious army before the invention of razors or discovery of clippers. There were whiskers of every length, shape and color. The beards were popular with the crowd of thousands of spectators, but not always so with the sweethearts and wives. With the women, it is only fair to remark now, these highly variegated types have been regarded as near grounds for divorce and the breaking of engagements. It is authoritatively reported that more than one love nest narrowly escaped being hopelessly wrecked through the determination of the Whiskerinos..." (May 27, 1922, *Sacramento Bee*.)

The Whiskerino contest raised more than $7,000 with all the people paying to see the contestants. C. C. Bennett was the winner of the $49 prize for the best beard growth since March 17; his beard measured one and eleven-sixteenths inches.

The old-growth beards were displayed and officially measured. Though Zack was assumed to be the favorite, a surprise was in store for the crowd. A North Dakota newspaper had learned about the celebration and told Hans N. Langseth. He participated in the event and his beard measured 17 feet, quickly putting all other contestants to shame! Zack's official beard measurement that day was 11 feet 3 inches. Combing definitely took a toll on the beard's length. Hans Langseth was officially named the King of the Whiskerinos and Zack was declared the Prince, later to be known as the Crown Prince. They ruled supreme for the week of the festivities.

According to the *Sacramento Bee*, King Langseth was "taken to the Mining Town, shown the Whiskers Palace, and had read to him a proclamation making him King of the Whiskerinos." An engraved gold medal was presented to him by Governor W. D. Stephens of California and many group photos were taken.

Zachary Wilcox with Hans Langseth, ca. 1922, Days of '49, Men with the Longest Beards. 1980/04/03, Arthur H. McCurdy Collection, Sacramento Archives & Museum Collection Center.

Clyde Seavey, Zack T. Wilcox, and Irvin Engler. Private Collection. Printed by permission from Meade Simpson.

Days of '49 Celebration, King of the Whiskerinos Hans Langseth (taller man with beard) and Crown Prince Zachary Taylor Wilcox (shorter man with beard). 1980/04/02, Arthur H. McCurdy Collection, Sacramento Archives & Museum Collection Center.

Langseth may also have started growing his beard for warmth. Born in Norway, Langseth came to America in 1876. He worked as a farmer during the cold winters in Minnesota and Iowa then later settled in North Dakota, becoming a land speculator. Hans had noticed that whiskers normally tended to break off at waist length but those under the chin could be grown much longer. He grew his whiskers for fifty years just to see how long they would grow. Like Zack, he kept his whiskers wrapped around a stick, placed in a bag, and tucked in his vest. For a short time he joined Ringling Brothers Circus, displaying his long beard. Preparation for these exhibitions necessitated a full combing by a barber, which could cost him up to $50. Langseth soon became disillusioned with people's skepticism that his whiskers were indeed authentic. He also had a sore chin from members of the crowd who would reach out and pull his whiskers to see if they were real. After only a few appearances, he returned to life in North Dakota where people knew he was genuine. He was once asked if his wife objected to his long beard. Apparently he already had the beard when they married and it was never a problem.

Crown Prince of the Whiskerinos

Hans Langseth, King of the Whiskerinos. Photo printed with permission from the Institute for Regional Studies, NDSU, Fargo (Folio 13.1).

Whiskerino Club members with Kings with the longest beards, ca. 1922, Left to Right: Jos. Herspring (kneeling), H. E. Diggles, Irvin Engler, king with longest beard, Clyde Seavey, Prince with second longest beard, Art Dudley, an employee of Van Voorhies Co., Arthur H. McCurdy (kneeling). 1980/04-04, Arthur H. McCurdy Collection, Sacramento Archives & Museum Collection.

The Days of '49 Celebration was not without rivalry among the groups participating. One *Sacramento Bee* article read, "Whiskerinos to have Rival Hair-Raisers in '49 Fete Rodeo." The rodeo planners made assurances that this would be one of the greatest events ever held in the West. W. I. Elliott, Chairman of the Rodeo Committee, complained to the Directors of the Chamber of Commerce that the Whisker movement was getting all the '49 publicity. He declared that the rodeo was going to furnish some hair-raising stunts that would attract thousands. With such events as the chariot races, the crowds were not disappointed.

Chariot Race Finish. Simpson team first place. Private Collection. Reprinted by permission from Meade Simpson.

Top Photo: Abe Lefton driving. Abe Lefton was a famous rodeo announcer who was inducted into the Rodeo Hall of Fame in 1990. He starred in several movies including, *Melody Trail* (1935) and *The Old Corral* (1937). Bill Elliott waving. Simpson Team.

Photo Below: Simpson Team in Days of '49 Parade. Photographs from Private Collection. Reprinted by permission from Meade Simpson.

The celebration in Sacramento was a great success with the parade, rodeo, Mining Town, and many other festivities. The Days of '49 Celebration lasted for six days and attendance estimates were as high as 100,000 people. At the end of the first five days of the celebration, the event had already raised $69,432. Though the Whiskerinos and whisker contests were a highlight, the real heroes of the celebration were the early California settlers and miners—pioneers like Charles S. Bell, who was one of the few remaining to tell the stories of pioneer times in California.

Excerpts of a letter Charles Bell sent to the *Sacramento Bee* (April 1, 1922):

I am a '49er, having crossed the plains with my parents at that time and with an ox team. Where now are great States of this Union was then the tireless expanse of prairie land then thought unfit for habitation. In the chimerical view of those days, mossed over by long vanishing time, it stands as a glimmer in the memory.

The Indian himself scuds phantom-like in spectral form, fleeing in shadowy way to his happy hunting ground his forefathers had molded by long traditions into his being. The great herd of buffalo no longer goes in thunder flight across the prairie.

The lean lanky prairie wolf no longer sits upon his haunches in some deepening shadow, making the night hideous with his yelping. All this vast wilderness has been transformed by the advance of civilization. Where there was immense wilderness now stands cities, great grain fields, superb villas, grand schoolhouses and magnificent State houses. The scream of the locomotive whistle reverberates through the narrow gorges of the Sierra Nevadas and Rocky Mountain canyons, now the delight of the tourist who looks from windows of palace cars, enraptured by the grandeur of nature that is before them.

No phantom disturbs their equanimity. The hush of the eternal silence disturbs them not. No tears burst from watery eyelids as those of the pioneer as they gather in solemn concourse about their silent deal to pay them the last sad tribute where they bury them under the prairie sod.

Individually I am standing with one foot upon the tombstone of the immortal pioneer and with the other upon the steps of the State Capitol. I turn in regret, looking backward upon the great mass of people, cosmopolitan in character, moving like ants, going here and there, digging and seeking for gold.

The great immense prairie of wild flowers variegated in color carpeting the virgin soil, is no longer to be seen. Occasionally a native wild flower steals in beside the path that has driven them from the wildness of California and bursts out in all its original beauty. The antelope, Mexican cattle, and the grizzly bear are no longer here. The Mexican vaquero, the denizen of all this wildness, I see in spectral form riding his tireless broncho into a waveless sea of immensity of space.

I turn now upon the steps of the State Capitol, one amongst the grandest in this Union, and salute with my pioneer hat the Native Sons and Daughters in the accomplishments that they have made or are before them.

At night as I cast my eyes over the great city burnished by electric lights as a great constellation of effective efficiency, men and women garbed in vestal fire of youth, go along the streets with pridely tread. Sutter's Fort stands ghostly in the murky distance, General

Sutter standing in effigy, beyond his kindly Swiss face beaming out of the immortal past, offering you this grand patrimony of a bursting empire that is before you.

I turn now and salute you, my young friends, as one of the retreating figures of the Days of '49, for only an atom of that great throng is left to tell a tale. The white tombstones of some rest at night, in shimmering moonlight sheer before you and many more sleep under a starry film in unmarked graves and under unmarked sod, never to rise again.

They are the retreating shadows that naught but imagination can replace. The orange blossoms perfume the air above the damp sod wherein they sleep and in solemn silence they are sleeping forever.

After the celebration, many citizens of Sacramento wanted to permanently keep the Mining Town and other facets of the Days of '49 Celebration. The answer from the city and the Chamber of Commerce was no. Their plan was that there would be a grand "flourish," then when all was done and the final guests had gone home, all remnants of the celebration would be virtually erased, paving the way for the future of this great city. As the new Chamber of Commerce declared via the *Sacramento Bee* on May 17, 1922, "Everybody on their toes Monday morning with a shave and a haircut ready to push Sacramento ahead." "Clean faces will take the place of once proud whiskers; sombreros will give way to straw hats, and summer suits will displace red shirts and bandannas." And with that, the outward appearance of the celebration was over. The motto generated for the event, however, outlasted the city's decree and the "Romance of California" remains in the minds of many to this day.

Opening of New Southern Pacific Depot, ca. 1924, man in front row (in center of line of women) is Arthur McCurdy. Steam engine is the C. P. Huntington No. 1. 1980/04/07, Arthur H. McCurdy Collection, Sacramento Archives & Museum Collection Center.

## Chapter Seven
## A Higher Calling

In the words that appeared in the *Sacramento Bee,* September 24, 1923, "For Zach, alive to the possibilities of traditions which may attach to his whiskers long after he has passed to that bourne (sic) where presumably whiskers might become entangled in the strings of his harp, has made provision for their preservation by bequeathing the luxuriant growth to the Whiskerinos of Sacramento." Plans were made for Zack's whiskers to be removed in accordance with his will upon his death. The beard was to be preserved in a glass case as a historical relic, "a symbol of what a man can do if the barbers let him alone and a striking memorial of the Days of '49." The plans were made for the continuation of this grand adventure as early as 1923, when Zack set down a will to bequeath his beard to the Whiskerinos. More than the final instructions of the Crown Prince, however, Zack's will embodied the altruistic optimism that Sacramento strove to capture in its Days of '49 Celebration.

*...to perpetuate the customs of the early settlers of the State of California, and the early history of the State of California, and to promote a spirit of loyalty toward them, and to perpetuate the memory of those whose sagacity, energy and enterprise induced them to settle in and become the founders of the Golden West...*

—Zachary Taylor Wilcox, Last Will and Testament

## Chapter Eight
## Zack's Final Lessons To His Subjects

As was apparent in his whisker will, Zack loved California. He relished the history of the Gold Rush and its enterprising pioneers. It was important to him that the State Legislature of California saw fit to pass Gold Discovery Day. Equally important was his desire that students be educated about the history of the early settlers of California. Though Zack made Carson City his home, a love for California was always in his heart. He did not want those Californians and all they endured to ever be forgotten.

**Among his last wishes was a desire to give to children:**

"the flowers of the field," "the blossoms of the woods with the right to play among them freely," "the banks of the brooks," "the golden sands beneath the waters thereof," "the odors of the willows," "the white clouds that float high over the largest trees in the world," "long days to be merry in," "the night and the moon and the train of the Milky Way to wonder at," "ideal fields…pleasant waters…all streams and ponds," "meadows with the clover blossoms and butterflies thereof," "the squirrels and birds and echoes and strange noises," "each his own place at the fireside at night," "their imaginary world," "stars of the sky, the red roses by the wall, the bloom of the California poppy," "the sweet strains of music," "inspiring sports of rivalry…disdain of weakness," "confidence in their own strength," "lasting friendships and possessing companions." And he wished to leave for those no longer children, "Memory…the happiness of old age, with the love and gratitude of their children until they fall asleep."

## Chapter Nine

## The Last Word

On December 31, 1926, the plans Zachary had outlined in his whisker will were put into motion. Zachary had passed away and now it was time for others to decide how his instructions would be carried out. Controversy ruled the day as the Whiskerinos of Sacramento, friends, and funeral directors in Carson City debated what was to be done. Judge Elijah Carson Hart, of Sacramento, was executor of the will. It was determined by Judge Hart that the will was indeed a valid one and that the Whiskerinos were entitled to the beard. The will had been legally signed, and was witnessed by G. E. Kitzmeyer and John M. Chartz, both of Carson City.

Zack's friends strongly protested the whisker removal and felt that his beard, which he had nurtured and enjoyed for so long, should accompany him to the grave. The funeral planning was obviously very emotional with this added controversy.

The Whisker Club made plans for a delegation to attend Zack's funeral and return to Sacramento with the whiskers. A committee consisting of J. L. Tucker, H. E. Diggles and J. M. Higgins planned to leave for Carson City as representatives of the club. There was no clear plan, however, as to what they would do with the whiskers once they obtained them.

The Whiskerinos envisioned the beard ultimately being placed in a glass box then being put on display at Sutter's Fort. A tentative plan was formed to meet the box containing the whiskers at the Southern Pacific station, in Sacramento, put them on a truck, then take them to the State Capitol. Plans were made for the strangest parade ever to be held in Sacramento.

An article was written stating that "A few hours before the final words, consigning him to the dust, were spoken, the wish expressed in his will that the Sacramento Whiskerinos Club become perpetual custodian of his most-prized possession was recognized. The undertakers clipped the famous fifteen-foot beard and put it in a box for shipment to Sacramento." The article went on to say, "They buried Zach in the town where nearly three-quarters of a century ago he sprouted and carefully nurtured the first of what was to become the world's second longest set of whiskers. There will be speeches and music and all that sort of thing for a fifteen-foot beard may be sneezed through but not at." (Jan. 3, 1927, *Sacramento Bee*.)

The final goodbye for Zack was held at the undertaking parlors of Kitzmeyer, Oliver, and Kenny. The funeral was under the direction of the G.A.R. and Women's Relief Corps. Services were conducted by the Independent Order of Odd Fellows. Zack was honored for his Civil War service by many friends and a few remaining members of the Grand Army of the Republic. "At the grave the Legion boys gave the old soldier the last military rites with taps." (Carson City *Daily Appeal*.)

But the final moments at his grave were not the final chapter of Zack's story. The saga continued and continues to this day. Headlines soon appeared in Sacramento: "Fifteen-Foot Beard Held By Undertaker Becoming White Elephant" and "Zach's Whiskers Proving Burden to Whiskerinos." Members of the Whiskers Club were laden with good intentions for the beard to become a lasting part of California's legacy at Sutter's Fort, but state officials had other notions. Protests were lodged with the officials of Sutter's Fort. The argument was to be put before the Board of Control and possibly the Grand Lodge of Native Sons.

Meanwhile, the undertakers in Carson City were frustrated and remained without clear direction as to what to do with the beard. They made a decision to hold onto the whiskers until they got official approval from Sacramento. Emotions seemed to be running high between the funeral directors in Carson City and the Whisker Club. Harry Diggles, Vice Chief of the Whiskerinos, when told of the undertakers' attitude, stated, "We're not going to send for them for a few days anyway." (Jan. 8, 1927, the *Sacramento Bee.)*

# Zach's Whiskers Proving Burden To Whiskerinos

## Fifteen-Foot Beard Held By Undertaker Becoming White Elephant

JUST what will become of the fifteen-foot beard of the late Zach T. Wilcox, crown prince of the local Whiskerino Club, became a question to-day that the state's highest officials will probably have to answer.

The beard was cut from Zach's chin last week a few hours before he was buried in compliance with a request in his will that his most prized possession become the property of the Sacramento club.

To-day a wee bit of doubt crept into the plans of the Whiskerinos for putting the whiskers in a glass case at Sutter's Fort. With several protests entered against the plan and with a new state administration in charge of the fort, the Whiskerino officials want to consult with the board of control before making definite arrangements.

Meanwhile the undertakers at Carson City, Nev., where Zach was buried, have the whiskers and are worried about what to do with them. They have received no word of authority from the club and will hold the whiskers until they get it. So much was indicated in a long distance conversation this morning.

"We're not going to send for them for a few days, anyway," said Harry Diggles, vice chief of the Whiskerinos, when informed of the undertaker's attitude. Diggles said the club would consult the board of control and probably trustees of the grand lodge of Native Sons.

*Sacramento Bee*, Jan. 8, 1927.

## Chapter Ten
## "A Few Days Anyway" and Some 80 Years Later

Harry Diggles may or may not have given the funeral home the final word as to what should be done with the famous whiskers. A decision may never have been made, with the issue left in discussion in perpetuity. Continued searches of newspapers and archives in Sacramento and Carson City have revealed no significant information. The mortuary in Carson City no longer exists and records have not been located that tell of Zack's funeral or the dispensation of the whiskers. Sutter's Fort has no records of the plan, the protests, or a final decision made by the administrators.

It seems that perhaps Zack's friends knew best after all. Or did they? If Zack had been buried with his whiskers, the story would have ended there and passed silently into history. Instead, there are many questions. Where are those whiskers today? Did the whiskers remain in a box at the funeral home in Carson City until lost or destroyed? Were they ever displayed as Zack wished them to be as a historical relic of the Golden Days? Is Carson City still awaiting word from Sacramento, or are the whiskers sitting in a box in an attic? Did someone take the wooden box to Zack's final resting place, push aside the sands of the Silver State, and let his whiskers be reunited with him forever?

What happened to the famous beard may never be known. The search for it, however, revealed not only the history of a missing beard, but the story of an interesting, compassionate man. In retrospect, the purpose of the whisker search may have been to lead to Zack's life story, his writings, and the story of the Whiskers Club of Sacramento.

## Chapter Eleven

## **The Final Stop**

Zack is now at rest in Lone Mountain Cemetery, in Carson City, Nevada.

His grave is dutifully cared for by the Sons of Union Veterans of the Civil War.

Photo by Carolyn Mirich.

Photo by Herbert Rickards. Printed with permission.

Photo by Herbert Rickards. Printed with permission.

Zack rests near a beautiful memorial recently built to honor the Veterans of the Civil War. It is assumed he was the last to be born into his family and, after a long interesting life, the last to die. Zack never married and remained a free, eccentric spirit throughout his life with close ties to his siblings and their families.

Zachary's brother, George, is also buried in the Civil War section of the cemetery in Carson City. Andrew is beside Zachary. These three brothers who were together through the Civil War and the journey west are together again.

Zack's brother, John, died September 13, 1914, in Flint, Michigan. Silas Wilcox died in 1899 in Whitingham, Vermont. His sister, Sally Elmira, married a Mr. Winchester. She lived and died in Lakeport, New Hampshire. Sister Fiducia (or Phildelia) married Hosea Dix. It is not known where she lived or died.

Hans Langseth on right displaying beard. 1981/01/1240, Sacramento Photography Survey Collection, Sacramento Archives & Museum Collection Center.

The King of the Whiskerinos, Hans Langseth, died in Kensett, Iowa, in 1927. When Hans Langseth died, his beard measured 18'6".

Apparently Langseth also chose to give up his beard on his final day. His beard was kept for years and was found in an attic chest in 1967. It was donated to the Smithsonian Institution in Washington, D.C. The beard was on display at the National Museum of Natural History until the Physical Anthropology Hall was dismantled in 1991.

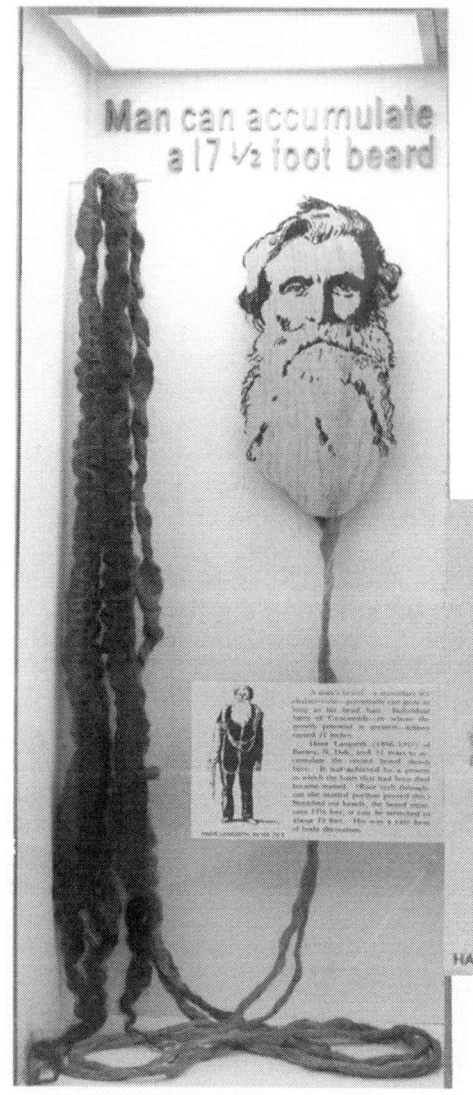

Image Courtesy of the Physical Anthropology Division, National Museum of Natural History, Smithsonian Institution, Catalog #387863.

British Pathe shot a newsreel of the king and crown prince, which survives to this day. It is titled *The End of the Chase*. The short film shows Hans displaying his beard. It also shows Hans and Zack standing on a bridge together. Hans demonstrated how he wrapped his beard and tucked it into his coat. (See British Pathe in the Bibliography for the location of the newsreel.)

## EPILOGUE

The Whiskers Club, which began as early as 1921, was still together to celebrate another Days of '49 Celebration in 1929. The original documents of the Whisker and Whiskerette Clubs stated that the clubs were intended to exist for a period of fifty years. The club members hoped to capitalize on the publicity they received from the days of Zack and Hans. In November 1922, the Whisker Club vowed to continue by electing 49 new directors. The Whiskerinos had a busy year in 1923. They held a successful party at Joyland Park, in Sacramento. Joyland Park was an amusement park built in the early 1890s. It featured a giant roller coaster and acts that included diving horses. The same year, more than 500 Whiskerinos and Whiskerettes attended celebrations of the Dons of Peralta in Oakland, where there were parades and barbecue feasts.

Judge Hart, executor of the whisker will, was appointed Chief Whiskerino in 1924. The club tried to buy an old fire engine, which would have presumably been for use in parades and other events. The Whiskerette Club was also very active at this time, staging competitive Virginia reel dances. In the year 1925, the club expressed an interest in purchasing the film the "Pony Express." It is not known if the Whiskerinos had appeared in this film. Few original films from this era still exist.

While the Whiskerinos and Whiskerettes partook of many social events, they also managed to do charity work as well. Approximately $7,000 was raised during the Days of '49. In 1926, the Whiskerinos donated $500 to an orphanage building fund. They also wanted to erect a monument to Alexander H. Willard of the Lewis & Clark expedition. There were undoubtedly many other charitable causes taken up by these groups. The Whiskerinos also dabbled in politics. They were supporters of State Senator J. M. Inman in his attempt to have the legislature designate January 24 as Gold Discovery Day—an occasion to be observed in all the schools of the State of California.

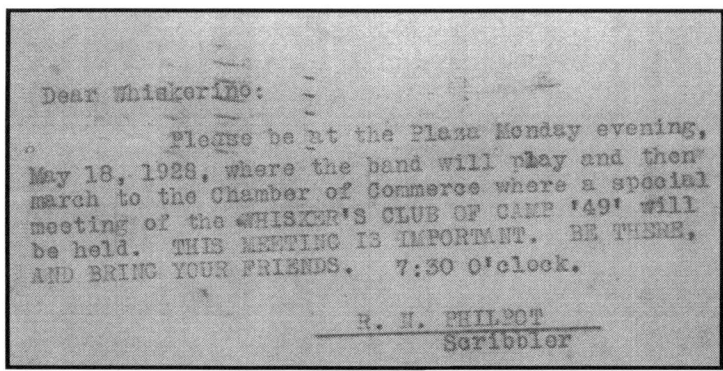

Courtesy of Department of Special Collections, Stanford University Libraries, Stanford, California. Harry C. Peterson Papers, ca. 1880–1944, Collection M0649, Box 2, Folder 40.

In 1939, a special ten-car train left Southern Pacific Station in Sacramento for Coloma, California. On this train was a party of Whiskerinos. They were celebrating the anniversary of John Marshall's discovery of gold.

The main intent of the Whiskerinos was to cultivate a continuity with the ambitions of their 1849 predecessors, a sentiment well represented by their Crown Prince. Zack was an ideal icon for the Whiskerinos and for Sacramento in 1922. Not only was Zack's will characteristic of the civic integrity manifested in the Days of '49 Celebration but, Zack's life was a testament to the enduring character of the American West. This was something that the Whiskerinos sought to uphold and emulate. What lives on all these years later, is the legacy of a kindly, dignified, well-loved gentleman who served his country willingly, knew how to enjoy his long life, and exemplified the pioneering spirit of the American West. This spirit is what Sacramento, in 1922, recognized and celebrated.

Photo of Zachary Wilcox, ca. 1902. Nevada Historical Society, Carson City, Nevada.

Photo of Zachary Wilcox, ca. 1902, in front of Benton's Stable. Nevada Historical Society, Carson City, Nevada.

## Whiskers Alive

The cultivation of whiskers is still sport in many circles. Modern-day whisker contests continue to provide both fun and funds for charitable organizations. There are local whisker clubs and world competitions. Reasons for growing beards and creative moustaches are as varied as the whiskers themselves—religion, fashion, manliness, mourning, hiding scars, warmth, attention, tradition, dislike of shaving, or pioneer celebrations.

The rules vary from one competition to another. The competitions have numerous classes, much like the contest in the Days of '49. This gives each participant the opportunity to compete with those who have a style similar to theirs. Judging is done much like in the Olympics. In the world competitions there are seven judges and the highest and lowest scores are eliminated. Each judge awards points from five to ten, with half points possible based on their opinion of which beard or moustache looks best. Judging is done by size, grooming, and how the facial hair fits the competitor's face. Costumes often accompany the contestant in order to show off the beard or moustache entered in the competition. Many contestants feel the addition of a costume adds to the chance of winning.

The following summary of the moustache and beard classes for modern events was furnished by Bruce Roe, of the Whisker Club of Bremerton, Washington, who also holds the position of president for the World Beard and Moustache Association.

## MOUSTACHE CLASSES

NATURAL    ENGLISH    IMPERIAL    DALI    HUNGARIAN    CHINESE

- **Natural-** No aids allowed! With the exception of Port Wine. All hairs grow from above and up to a fingers breadth beyond the end of the lips.
- **English-** Narrow; the hairs grow from above but not beyond the end of the lips, are swung outward extremely long and slightly upwards, points slightly raised.
- **Imperial-** Bushy; the hairs grow from above but not beyond the end of the lips, small with the points turned up.
- **Dali-** Narrow; the hairs grow from above but not beyond the end of the lips, long points in an arch or steeply directed upwards.
- **Hungarian-** Big, Bushy; The hairs grow from above but not beyond the end of the lips, pulled outwards and upwards.
- **Chinese-** Growth allowed two finger breadths below the corner of the mouth, points long and downwards.
- **Freestyle-** All other moustaches that do not correspond with given classes.

## BEARD CLASSES

**CHIN BEARDS**      **FULL BEARDS**

NATURAL   MUSKETEER   IMPERIAL     NATURAL   GARIBALDI   VERDI

Chin beards must have a minimum separation of one inch between sideburn and beard.

- **Natural-** No aids allowed! The moustache may be styled with Port Wine but no wax, spray or gel.
- **Musketeer-** Small pointed beard clearly separated from moustache. Moustache styled to narrow upward arch or straight to the side.
- **Imperial-** Hairs grown only from the upper lip and cheeks. Chin shaved with moustache arched upward.
- **Freestyle-** All beards with minimum separation that do not correspond to other classes.

- **Natural-** No aids allowed! The moustache may be styled with Port Wine but no wax, spray or gel.
- **Garibaldi-** Broad, full, and round below with integrated moustache. No aids allowed!
- **Verdi-** Round below, relatively short, and cheek slightly shaved. Moustache styled.
- **Freestyle-** All full beards not corresponding with other classes.

A challenge for modern whisker clubs might be inspiring an entire city to cultivate whiskers as Sacramento proved was possible during the good ol' Days of '49 in 1922.

## DAYS OF '49 MEMORABILIA

Celebrate Days of '49. Published with permission. Sacramento Public Library, Sacramento Room.

## DAYS OF '49 CELEBRATION        SACRAMENTO, MAY 23rd to 28th

THE DAYS OF '49! What vivid memories those few words bring to mind! Prairie schooners flocking westward; eager souls plunging on to fields of newly-found fortune; vessels rounding the Horn and streaming toward the golden goal in Northern California; frenzied miners sifting the earth for nuggets and gold dust; richness and ruggedness, gaiety and glamour, rashness and recklessness; a seething maelstrom of money-mad humans; a picture colorful and turbulent yet softened by the spirit of comradeship in adventure and tempered with the tone of hearty hospitality. In all history there is nothing to equal this Great Romance of California.

SACRAMENTO, California's Capital, was the center of this human vortex. Sutter Fort was the rendezvous of the frenzied throngs. Sacramento, born of the Gold Rush hysteria, is proud of its picturesque origin and brings those days back to life in a great annual celebration—a National event, as widespread in interest and just as alluring as the period of history it reproduces.

THE CURTAIN of the Past is thrown aside. You see the Romance of California revivified, with all its glowing color and bristling action. Spread before you is a typical '49 Mining Town such as inspired the pen of Bret Harte. Original "Roaring Camp" could not be more realistic. Scores of cities and communities, at a cost of many thousands of dollars, contributed to its construction. At the State Fair Grounds will be staged America's greatest Wild West contest, 300 daredevil riders competing for $10,000 in prizes. There will be a Gold Rush parade, made up of ox-teams, prairie schooners, stage coaches, miners, burros and Indians—the strangest cavalcade in history; Indian villages; pioneer day athletic events; historical dramas and pageants; Indian battles and scores of other features all woven into a living, kaleidoscopic panorama depicting the Great Romance that is synonymous with California.

### INFORMATION.

The "Days of '49" Celebration opens in Sacramento on Tuesday, May 23rd, and will continue to and including Sunday, May 28th.

"Founding of Sacramento" and Indian Battle on opening day; formal opening of Mining Town; "Governor's Inaugural Ball—Days of '49" in evening.

Wild West Contest Wednesday to Sunday, both days inclusive.

Mining Town, with scores of unusual attractions, open every day and night.

"Days of '49 Styles Show" Wednesday evening. Prizes for best costumes typical of Gold Rush days.

"Gold Rush Parade" Friday morning.

Pioneer day athletic events and parades every morning.

Historical dramas and allegories, operation of first transcontinental railroad engine, championship shoot and other special events during the week.

Transcontinental railroad rates effective May 15th. Ask your ticket agent for the reduced fare. Local excursion rates from all California points.

Sacramento cordially invites you and will bend every effort to make your visit enjoyable, delightful and impressive.

Under the Management of
SACRAMENTO CHAMBER of COMMERCE

Chamber of Commerce Brochure. Published with permission, Sacramento Public Library, Sacramento Room.

---

### Miner's Pot-Luck

Shirt-tail Bend Rib-warmer

High-grade Olives        Texas Hill Onions

Coon Hollow Pickles

Bumsquizzle 'em a la '49 with Webertown Murphys
Spanish Ravine Nuggets        Riffle Biscuits

Hangtown Tailings

Cemented Gravel        Quartz Rocks, assorted

Marshall's Delight en Tasse

Miner's Pot-Luck Menu. Published with permission, Sacramento Public Library, Sacramento Room.

## A Celebration Without Parallel

VISUALIZING the most sensational chapter of American History, the "Days of '49" celebration in Sacramento is original, distinctive and positively without parallel.

THROUGHOUT the "Gold Rush" area of California, cities and towns have pooled their resources and efforts to bring before the eyes of the Nation, in a prodigious display, thrilling episodes that have made the "Days of '49" a household expression.

MEN thoroughly acquainted with the life and customs of that period have combed the whole mining territory for material and relics that were actually a part of its history—prairie schooners; ox-carts; stage coaches; gold scales; long-toms; muskets; miners' equipment; gambling outfits; cannon—and countless other articles which, when assembled, furnish an attraction which alone would be worth a trip across the continent.

UNDER the direction of experts, a committee of 1,000 is working out scores of features—a series of spectacular events for each day—a continuous chain of activity, entertainment and thrills.

THIS folder gives but a glimpse of the event.

CALIFORNIA'S State Capital, Sacramento, in its entirety, will be turned back to the "Days of '49", throughout the length and breadth of its fourteen square miles.

NOTE: The Sacramento Chamber of Commerce will send you an attractive historical booklet "THE ROMANCE OF CALIFORNIA" which tells of the Gold Days, if you address "Days of '49" Committee, Chamber of Commerce, Sacramento, California.

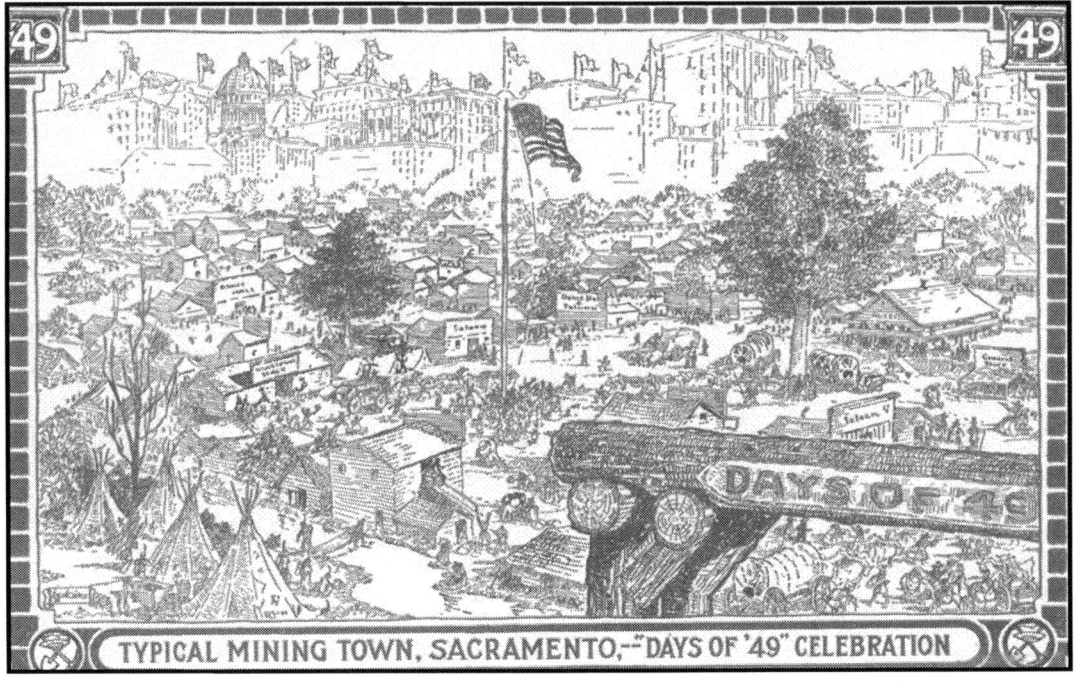

TYPICAL MINING TOWN, SACRAMENTO,—"DAYS OF '49" CELEBRATION

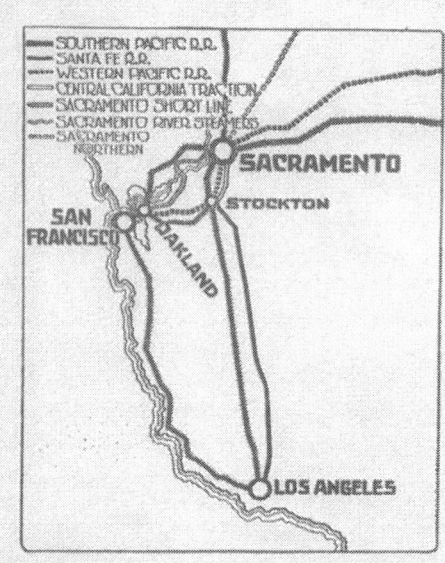

# BE A '49er

SACRAMENTO extends to you a cordial invitation to come back to the "Days of '49." Transcontinental railroad excursion rates are effective May 15th. You benefit by a substantial reduction in fare and arrive in Sacramento in time to enjoy the entire celebration.

▯ ▯ ▯

EXEMPLIFYING the Spirit of Western Hospitality which was characteristic of the Days of Gold, Sacramento not only invites you with sincere cordiality, but assures you that every effort will be exerted to make your visit so thoroughly enjoyable and delightfully impressive that it will always linger in your memory.

Management SACRAMENTO CHAMBER of COMMERCE

"GOLD RUSH" PARADE—SACRAMENTO—"DAYS OF '49" CELEBRATION

# Romantic Days Revivified

YOU'VE longed to realize your vision of the Days of '49. Make that wish come true! Come back to the "Days of '49" in Sacramento, May 23-28, 1922.

SACRAMENTO, Capital of California, was the hub of that seething maelstrom of gold-seekers—the "Forty-Niners." The "Days of Old, the Days of Gold" were the foundation of California history.

AND now Sacramento brings those days back to life with all their color and glamour, in the greatest of all annual celebrations---remarkably realistic and historically correct in every detail. The city's principal business streets again become thoroughfares of the Sacramento of '49.

OLD mining towns spring into life, radiant with the spirit of '49; original Sutter Fort is again the trading post and rendezvous of frenzied gold-seekers. The founding of Sacramento---discovery of gold---rush to the "Gold Diggin's"---clashes with Indians---these are among the episodes to be enacted in pageant, parade and drama.

PRAIRIE schooners replace street cars; dance halls are strung along the winding streets; white collars and modern footwear give way to red flannel and miners' boots; real gold nuggets are in circulation, washed out as they were in the Days of '49.

THE transformation will be complete--- a living, kaleidoscopic depiction of "THE ROMANCE of CALIFORNIA." And you may be a part of it.

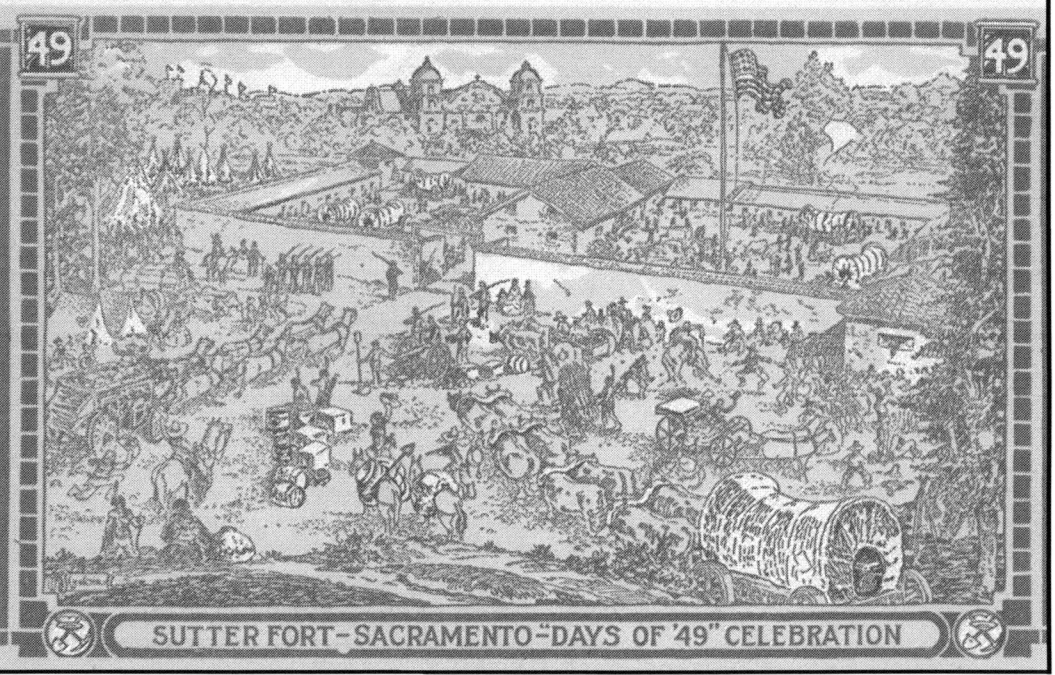

SUTTER FORT—SACRAMENTO—DAYS OF '49" CELEBRATION

# Bizarre, Spectacular, Inspiring

WHEN you arrive in Sacramento you find the Curtain of the Past thrown aside. Spread before you is a typical '49 Mining Town brought into being by the united effort of scores of cities and communities in the old gold diggings districts. Here you may live the life of the true Forty-Niner amid surroundings just as alluring as the period of history which is reproduced.

YOU marvel at the realism of the living picture—bizarre, spectacular, inspiring. On every side is a new surprise—a thrill quite unlike any you have ever experienced.

EACH day of the celebration is marked with unique cavalcades—strange processions bringing before your eyes the whole romantic history of the Gold Rush. Here you feel the thrill that inspired the pen of Bret Harte. You mingle with characters that seem to have stepped out of his books and witness scenes that grip you with their realism.

HISTORICAL celebrities—Fremont, the pathfinder; Kit Carson, the boys' hero; Sutter, the adventurer; Marshall, the discoverer of gold—live again in this commemorative drama, and are the central figures of the picture.

THE unusual panorama spreads over the city to the State Fair Grounds where America's greatest Wild West Contest—a $20,000 feature—will be presented by a matchless aggregation made up of hundreds of cowboys and Indians. Never before in history has such a sensational event been arranged.

THE life, customs, styles and characters of the Days of Gold are restored in this most unusual of National Celebrations. Your dream of the Days of '49 is made a reality.

Chamber of Commerce Brochure. Printed with permission, Sacramento Public Library, Sacramento Room.

Songsheet. Reprinted by permission from Sacramento Room, Sacramento Public Library. Lyrics follow.

*Hail! Hail! The gang's all here*

*Sacramento mine*

*Days of forty nine*

*Here's where the grizzly bear*

*Flags a welcome straight to you*

*S. A. C. R. A. M. E. N. T. O.*

## Chorus:

*"To Sacramento*

*Come on and help us*

*Push Father Time back to Forty nine*

*There'll be lots doing*

*And you'll be rueing*

*If you miss this grand old time*

*In Sacramento we're goin' to show you*

*Just how they lived and danced and dined*

*And wore their whiskers boots and bonnets too*

*In the good old days of Forty nine."*

*Oh boy the things you'll see*

*Bring your trusty gun*

*Bandits on the run*

*We'll live through history*

*Days when grandpa had his fun*

*Miners with tales of gold*

*To you they will unfold.*

*Sacramento Bee,* April 15, 1922.

# APPENDIX

Will of Zachary Taylor Wilcox.

Articles of Incorporation of the Whisker Club of Camp '49.

Articles of Incorporation of the Whiskerette Club of Camp '49.

IN THE NAME OF THE CROWN PRINCE WHISKERINO OF ALL WHISKERINOS:

I, ZACK WILCOX, of Carson City, Nevada, being of sound and disposing mind and memory, and not acting under duress, menace, fraud or undue influence of the Whiskers Club of Camp '49, a corporation of Sacramento City, California, or of any person whomsoever, nor of any kind whatsoever, and the Grand Jury of the Whiskerinos having returned its verdict that I have the second longest beard of any person in the whole world, to-wit: fourteen feet, and said verdict having been approved by the Chief Whiskerino of the Golden West, from whose decision there is no known appeal, his jurisdiction being extra-territorial, and wishing to assist in and encourage the spreading of the epidemic which raged in and around the Golden West in the year 1849, which, under microscopic examination, shows a peculiar fungus growth on the cultural tubes, which after incubation develops into an odd, hairy-like growth and which eventually develops into a luxuriant growth of whiskers, and having grown whiskers for a period of nigh unto forty-nine years, and wishing at this time to bequeath my whiskers to the Whiskers Club of Camp '49, a corporation of Sacramento City, California, and wishing to bequeath none other of my worldly goods under this will, do make, publish and declare this my last will and testament for the bequeathing of said whiskers, that is to say:

First: I direct that my body be decently buried with proper ceremony and regard to my rank as Crown Prince Whiskerino of all the world, and I direct that all Whiskerinos

1

hold a proper ceremony befitting my rank at Camp '49 at Sacramento City in the Golden West, and the Whiskers Club of Camp '49 conduct said ceremony and last rites;

Second: That part of my interests and property which is known to law and recognized in the sheep bound volumes as my property, I make no disposal of in this my will. I will make provisions for the disposal of the same in another will, and it is my wish that no will hereafter executed by me shall conflict with the provisions of this will, and that any will heretofore or hereafter executed by me will be considered an addenda to this will;

Third: My right to be Crown Prince Whiskerino of all the world being but a life estate, or until I shave my beard or some other human being grows a longer beard, is not at my disposal, the same having been granted to me without remainder or right of succession or inheritance, but with my title, real and personal property excepted, all else in the world I now proceed to devise and bequeath;

Fourth: I will, give, devise and bequeath unto the Board of Directors of the Whiskers Club of Camp '49, a corporation of Sacramento, California, my whiskers, to be held by them in trust for the Whiskers Club of Camp '49, and all of my subjects, the loyal Whiskerinos;

Fifth: I give to my subjects, and all members of the Whiskers Club of Camp '49 and all loyal Whiskerinos, in trust for their children, all and every, the flowers of the field and the blossoms of the woods, with the right to play among them freely according to the customs of '49, warning them at the same time against thistles and thorns; and I devise to my subjects the banks of the brooks of the region of '49 and the golden sands beneath the waters thereof, and the odors of the willows that dip therein, and the white clouds that float high over the largest trees in the world, which grow near Camp '49, and I leave the children of my subjects the long, long days to be merry in, in a thousand ways, and the night and the moon and the train of the Milky Way to wonder at, but subject nevertheless to the rights hereinafter given to lovers of the Golden West;

Sixth: I give and devise to boy whiskerinos jointly all the useful ideal fields and commons of '49 where ball may be played, all pleasant waters in and around Camp '49 where one may coast, and all streams and ponds around Camp '49 where one may fish, or where, when grim winter comes, one may skate, to have and to hold the same for the period of their boyhood; and all meadows with the clover blossoms and butterflies thereof, the woord sna their appurtenances, the squirrels and birds and echoes and strange noises, and all distant places which may be visited near Camp '49, together with the adventures there found. And I give to said boys of all Whiskerinos each his own place at the fireside at night with all pictures of the days of '49 that may be seen in the burning wood, to enjoy without let or hindrance and without any incumbrance or care;

Seventh: To lovers of the Days of '49 I devise their imaginary world, with whatever they may need, as the stars of the sky, the red roses by the wall, the bloom of the California poppy, the sweet strains of music, and aught else by which they may edesire to figure to each other the lastingness and beauty of their love;

Eighth: To young men whiskerinos jointly I devise and bequeath all boisterous, inspiring sports of rivalry; and I give to them the disdain of weakness and undaunted confidence in their own strength, though they are rude. I give them the power to make lasting friendships, and of possessing companions, and to them exclusively I give all merry songs and brave choruses of the days of '49, to sing with lusty voices;

Ninth: To those who are no longer children or youths or lovers, I leave memory, and I bequeath to them the volumes of the writings of Bret Harte, Joaquin Miller and Robert Louis Stevenson, and of the other poets and writers, if there be others, of the days of '49, to the end that they may live over again the days of '49 in the Golden West, freely and fully without tithe or diminution;

Tenth: To all my loved ones and all my subjects with snowy crowns, I bequeath the happiness of old age, with the love and gratitude of their children until they fall asleep;

Eleventh: To the good teachers who fully complied with an Act to establish Gold Discovery Day, passed by the State Legislature of the State of California making January 24th of each year Gold Discovery Day, being the anniversary of the discovery of gold in California, and who

4

include in the school work of said day suitable exercises and lessons having for their object instruction of the pupils as to the discovery of gold in California and the development of the resources of the State of California and to perpetuate the customs of the early settlers of the State of California, and the early history of the State of California, and to promote a spirit of loyalty toward them, and to perpetuate the memory of those whose sagacity, energy and enterprise induced them to settle in and become the founders of the Golden West, I hereby give and bequeath a long life and perpetual happiness;

Lastly: I hereby name and appointe the Chief Whiskerino of the Whiskers Club of Camp '49, a corporation, whomever he may be at the time of my death, as the executor of this will and testament. I hereby revoke any and all and every clause in any will, heretofore or hereafter made by me, wherein I attempt or attempted to bequeath my whiskers.

IN WITNESS WHEREOF I have hereunto set my hand and seal this ___17___ day of ___August___, 1923.

      ___Jack Wiley___ (SEAL)

The foregoing instrument, consisting of five pages besides this one, was, at the date hereof, by the said Zack Wilcox signed, sealed and published as his whisker will and testament in the presence of us, who at his request and in his presence and in the presence of each other, have subscribed our names as witnesses thereto.

*Geo. E. Kitzmeyer*

Residing at _Carson City, Nev._

*John M. Chartz*

Residing at _Carson City, Nev._

Last Will and Testament of Zachary Taylor Wilcox, Nevada Historical Society. Printed with permission.

ARTICLES OF INCORPORATION

OF

" WHISKERS CLUB OF CAMP '49 "

KNOW ALL MEN BY THESE PRESENTS:

That we, the undersigned, all of whom are citizens of the United States of America and residents of the State of California, have this day voluntarily associated ourselves together for the purpose of forming a corporation and incorporating under the laws of the State of California, a social, fraternal, benevolent and historical society,

AND WE HEREBY CERTIFY:

FIRST: That the name of said corporation shall be "Whiskers club of Camp '49";

SECOND: That the objects for which said corporation are formed are:-

To assist in the developement of the resouces of the region of the Golden West and to perpetuate the traditions and customs of 1849;

To collect and preserve information in connection with the early settlers and subsequent history of the Golden West;

To form such libraries and cabinets and pursue such literary and scientific objects, as may be determined, and in all appropriate matters to advance the interests and perpetuate the memory of those whose sagacity, energy and enterprise induced them to settle in and become the founders of the Golden West;

To promulgate the principles, teachings and objects of this order;

-1-

ARTHUR H. McCURDY
LAWYER
SACRAMENTO, CALIFORNIA

To encourage the growth of horny fibrous substance with a central medualla enclosing pigment cells which on the outside are scales like tiles on a roof, forming delicate lines on hair surfaces, transverse, oblique, or spiral;

To assist in and encourage the spreading of the epidemic which raged in and around the Golden West in the year 1849 which, under microscopic examination shows a peculiar fungus growth on the cultural tubes which after incubating develop into an odd, hairy-like growth which eventually develops into a luxuriant growth of whiskers;

When advisable, to organize and institute sub-ordinate clubs in the various cities or towns in the Golden West and to maintain supervision over such sub-ordinate bodies and clubs and their membership and according to the rules and discipline of said corporation and under the supervision of its officers to take charge of its buildings, estates, property and temporalities, not, however, for profit.

THIRD: That the place where the principle business of said corporation is to be transacted is Camp '49, Sacramento City, California.

FOURTH: That this corporation is not formed for the purpose of pecuniary profit and pecuniary profits are not the object of said corporation and the purpose of said corporation are other than pecuniary profit;

FIFTH: That the term for which said corporation is to exist is fifty years from and after the date of its incorporation.

SIXTH: That the number of directors of said corporation shall be twelve.

-2-

ARTHUR H. McCURDY
LAWYER
SACRAMENTO, CALIFORNIA

SEVEN: That the names and residences of the directors who are elected and appointed for the first year and to serve until the election and qualification of their successors are all of the undersigned as undersigned;

IN WITNESS WHEREOF, we have hereunto set our hands and seals in the 73rd year post '49 on the 18th day of May, A. D. 1922.

| NAMES | RESIDENCES. |
|---|---|
| Clyde L. Seavey | Sacramento, Cal. |
| H. E. Diggles | Sacramento, Cal. |
| John W. Callaon | Sacramento, Calif. |
| Norman H. Robotham | Sacramento, Cal. |
| Arthur H. McCurdy | Sacramento, Cal. |
| Ralph H. Lewis | Sacramento, California. |
| Harold J. McCurry | Sacramento, Calif. |
| Geo. V. Work | Sacramento, California |
| Jos. Herspring | Sacramento, California |
| Theodore N. Koening | Sacramento, Calif. |
| H. W. Funke | Sacramento, Cal. |
| C. C. Gupton | Sacramento, Cal. |

-3-

ARTHUR H. McCURDY
LAWYER
SACRAMENTO, CALIFORNIA

```
STATE OF CALIFORNIA    )
                       ) SS.
COUNTY OF SACRAMENTO   )

                    On this 18th day of May, 1922,
before me, J. S. Daly, a Notary Public in and for said County
and State, personally appeared
Clyde L. Seavey              Harold J. McCurry
H. E. Diggles                Geo. A. Work
John W. Callnon              Jos. Herspring
Norman H. Robotham           Theodore N. Koening
Arthur H. McCurdy            H. W. Funke
Ralph H. Lewis               C. C. Cupton,
known to me to be the persons whose names are subscribed to the
within instrument and articles of corporation, and they each for
themselves and not one for the other, duly acknowledged to me
that they each executed the same and that they each executed the
same as director of said corporation.
```

*J. S. Daly*
Notary Public in and for the
County of Sacramento, State of
California.

ARTHUR H. McCURDY
LAWYER
SACRAMENTO, CALIFORNIA

ARTICLES OF INCORPORATION

OF

"WHISKERETTE CLUB OF CAMP '49".

KNOW ALL WOMEN AND MEN BY THESE PRESENTS:

That we, the undersigned, all of whom are citizens of the United States of America and residents of the State of California, have this day voluntarily associated ourselves together for the purpose of forming a corporation and incorporating under the laws of the State of California, a social fraternal, benevolent and historical society,

AND WE HEREBY CERTIFY:

FIRST: That the name of said corporation shall be "Whiskerette Club of Camp '49".

SECOND: That the objects for which said corporation are formed are:

To perpetuate the memory, courage and sagacity of the brave mothers, daughters, wives and sweethearts who devoted their lives in the endeavor to settle and build the Golden West;

To perpetuate the memory of the women, girls and babies who were members of the famous "Donner Party";

To perpetuate the memory and history of all the towns, hamlets, cities, villages and camps of the Mother Lode;

To inculcate among its members, the democratic sociability of the early Pioneers of the Golden West;

To assist in settling and developing the region of the Golden West, and in particular, Sacramento, THE HEART OF

ARTHUR H. McCURDY
LAWYER
SACRAMENTO, CALIFORNIA

CALIFORNIA;

To encourage the reading of the works and writings of the authors of the early days of California, and in particular, the writings of Bret Harte;

To act as a Luncheon Club;

To teach the coming generation the art of cooking, to become more homelike and to build and develop more homes;

To encourage the purchase of, and use in all homes of all goods, wares and merchandise, sold and manufactured in Sacramento County so as to encourage the establishment of manufacturing plants in Sacramento County;

To act as an auxilliary to the Whiskers Club of Camp '49;

To assist in making Sacramento an inland seaport;

To assist, revive and encourage the mining industries in the Golden West and assist in making mining conventions held in Camp '49, Sacramento, Cal., a complete success;

To assist in the development of the resources of the region of the Golden West, and to perpetuate the traditions and customs of 1849, and early days of California;

To collect and preserve information in connection with the early settlers and subsequent history of the Golden West;

To form such libraries and cabinets and pursue such literary and scientific objects, as may be determined, and to all appropriate matters to advance the interests and perpetuate the memory of those whose sagicity, energy and enterprise induced them to settle in and become the founders of the Golden West;

To promulgate the principles, teachings and objects of this order;

When advisable, to organize and institute subordinate clubs in the various cities or towns in the Golden West, and to maintain supervision over such subordinate bodies or clubs and their membership, according to the rules and discipline of said corporation, and under the supervision of its officers to take charge of the buildings, estates, property and temporalities belonging to said corporation, not however, for profit.

THIRD: That the place where the principle business of said corporation is to be transacted is Camp '49, Sacramento, California.

FOURTH: That this corporation is not formed for the purpose of pecuniary profit and pecuniary profits are not the object of said corporation and the purpose of said corporation are other than pecuniary profit.

FIFTH: That the term for which said corporation is to exist is fifty years from and after the date of its incorporation.

SIXTH: That the number of directors of said corporation shall be forty-nine.

PROVIDED, that the corporate powers, business and property of said corporation may be exercised, conducted and controlled by the Board of Directors, consisting of such

ARTHUR H. McCURDY
LAWYER
SACRAMENTO, CALIFORNIA

number of directors as maybe provided in the Constitution or By-Laws of said Corporation hereafter adopted, and the said Corporation may, in its Constitution or By-Laws provide for the length of time the Directors or any number thereof shall act, and may in like manner provide that certain directors, or certain number of the Board of Directors, to be selected by the corporation or Board of Directors, in the mode and manner provided in the Constitution or By-Laws, shall act for any specified length of time or otherwise, as shall be in the constitution or By-Laws set forth.

SEVENTH: That the names and residences of the directors who are elected and appointed for the first year and to serve until the election and qualification of their successors are all of the undersigned, as undersigned.

EIGHTH: That during the days of 49, to wit, May 23rd to May 28th, 1922, the following document was issued by the Chief Whiskerino of the Golden West, as follows, to-wit:

"KNOW ALL MEN BY THESE PRESENTS, AND TO WHOM THESE PRESENTS SHALL COME, GREETINGS: SHUDDER.

An ultimatum that all persons afflicted with the new disease know as "Whiskeritis" must either join the "Whisker Club", where they can be properly supervised or be placed in quarantine, is hereby issued by the Chief Whiskerino of the Golden West residing at Camp '49;

If, after the issuance of these presents there be found any person disobeying this proclamation, I will punish the delinquent severely and will exercise no mercy.

  Tremble!  Be more careful!  Do not say bye and bye that you have had no notice!

  Being in favor of spreading the epidemic now raging in and around Sacramento in the County of Sacramento, California, which under microscopic examination shows a peculiar fungus growth on the culture tubes, which after incubating, developes into an odd hairy like growth which eventually develops into a luxuriant growth of whiskers;

  I HEREBY ISSUE THE FOLLOWING PRESENTS: This is to certify that Valla E. Parkinson has been duly invested with the Decree of Chief Whiskerette by order of the Whisker Club and is hereby given full power and authority to establish a Whiskette Club in Sacramento, County of Sacramento, California, with full and complete power and authority to establish a Kangaroo Court in said city or town, extra territorial;

  GIVEN AND GRANTED under my hand and seal this 18th day of May, 1922, at Camp '49, in the State of California.

     (signed) <u>C. L. SEAVEY</u>
          Chief Whiskerino of the
          Golden West"

SEAL.

and that the Whiskerette Club was duly formed and participated in the celebration of the Days of 49, to wit, May 23rd to May 28th, 1922.

ARTHUR H. McCURDY
LAWYER
SACRAMENTO, CALIFORNIA

NINTH: That the names and residences of the Directors who were elected and appointed for the first year, and to serve until election and qualification of their successors are as follows; to wit:

| NAMES | RESIDENCES |
|---|---|
| V. E. PARKINSON | SACRAMENTO, CALIFORNIA. |
| GENE B. KING | SACRAMENTO, CALIFORNIA. |
| SOPHIE NIELSEN | SACRAMENTO, CALIFORNIA. |
| BEULAH FITZGERALD | SACRAMENTO, CALIFORNIA. |
| MADELINE HERSPRING | SACRAMENTO, CALIFORNIA. |
| ADELLIA C. McCURDY | SACRAMENTO, CALIFORNIA |
| EDITH P. McCURDY | SACRAMENTO, CALIFORNIA |
| FLORA CRAWFORD | SACRAMENTO, CALIFORNIA |
| FLORENCE DELAHAUNTY | SACRAMENTO, CALIFORNIA |
| BERTHA R. PALMER | SACRAMENTO, CALIFORNIA |
| NELL D. FENTON | SACRAMENTO, CALIFORNIA |
| HAZEL GRAHAM | SACRAMENTO, CALIFORNIA |
| HANNAH HARDER | SACRAMENTO, CALIFORNIA |
| BESSIE R. ANAPOLSKY | SACRAMENTO, CALIFORNIA |
| GWEN L. ADAMS | SACRAMENTO, CALIFORNIA |
| NELLIE M. HEWS | SACRAMENTO, CALIFORNIA |
| ANNA ZIMMERMAN | SACRAMENTO, CALIFORNIA |
| BETTY OGDEN | SACRAMENTO, CALIFORNIA |
| ALVA S. ARCHER | SACRAMENTO, CALIFORNIA |
| MRS. EMMA NUNNELEY | SACRAMENTO, CALIFORNIA |
| MRS MARTHA ARCHER | SACRAMENTO, CALIFORNIA |
| MINNIE DUNN | SACRAMENTO, CALIFORNIA |
| MAE KAWKINS | SACRAMENTO, CALIFORNIA |
| TAIMA ZETTA WILBUR, | SACRAMENTO, CALIFORNIA |
| MISS ROE CALIFRO | SACRAMENTO, CALIFORNIA |
| BERNICE E. FAUSTMAN | SACRAMENTO, CALIFORNIA |
| MILDRED M. COOPER | SACRAMENTO, CALIFORNIA |
| MRS. ETHEL DAVIDSON | SACRAMENTO, CALIFORNIA |
| MRS. J. H. CHRISTIAN | SACRAMENTO, CALIFORNIA |
| MRS. LILLIAN SNIDER | SACRAMENTO, CALIFORNIA |
| MRS. ANNIE KUBEL | SACRAMENTO, CALIFORNIA |
| DORA PARKER (CUTTER) | SACRAMENTO, CALIFORNIA |
| MRS. A. J. KUSTER | SACRAMENTO, CALIFORNIA |
| BETTY KUSTER | SACRAMENTO, CALIFORNIA |
| TEDA HOSKING | SACRAMENTO, CALIFORNIA |
| REGINA M. STEWART | SACRAMENTO, CALIFORNIA |
| LUCIA M. ANDREWS | SACRAMENTO, CALIFORNIA |
| ELEANOR H. POSEY | SACRAMENTO, CALIFORNIA |
| LORETTA E. HIGGINS | SACRAMENTO, CALIFORNIA |
| JOSIE L. LASCANO | SACRAMENTO, CALIFORNIA |
| ETHEL FENTON | SACRAMENTO, CALIFORNIA |
| MRS. E. C. HART | SACRAMENTO, CALIFORNIA |
| MRS. ELSIE L. GREILICH | SACRAMENTO, CALIFORNIA |
| EDITH BROWN | SACRAMENTO, CALIFORNIA |
| MRS. MYRTLE GREER | SACRAMENTO, CALIFORNIA |
| VIVIAN E. POWERS | SACRAMENTO, CALIFORNIA |
| MARION E. MELLIN | SACRAMENTO, CALIFORNIA |
| MABEL MOXNESS | SACRAMENTO, CALIFORNIA |
| SERENA KARLHANG | SACRAMENTO, CALIFORNIA |

ARTHUR H. McCURDY
LAWYER
SACRAMENTO, CALIFORNIA

STATE OF CALIFORNIA     )
                        ) SS
COUNTY OF SACRAMENTO    )

On this 21st day of April, in the year one thousand nine hundred and twenty-four, before me Arthur H. McCurdy, a notary public in and for said County, personally appeared V. E. Parkinson, Gene B. King, Sophie Nielsen, Beulah Fitzgerald, Madeline Herspring, Adellia C. McCurdy, Edith P. McCurdy, Flora Crawford, Florence Delahaunty, Bertha R. Palmer, Nell D. Fenton, Hazel Graham, Hannah Harder, Bessie R. Anapolsky, Gwen L Adams, Nellie M. Hews, Anna Zimmerman Betty Ogden, Alva S. Archer, Mrs. Emma Nunneley, Mrs Martha Archer, Minnie Dunn, Mae Hawkins, Talma Zetta Wilbur, Miss Roe Califro, Bernice E. Faustman, Mildred M. Cooper, Mrs. Ethel Davidson, Mrs. J. H. Christian, Mrs. Lillian Snider, Mrs. Annie Kubel, Dora Parker (Cutter) Mrs. A. J. Kuster, Betty Kuster, Teda Hosking, Regina M. Stewart, Lucia M. Andrews, Eleanor H. Posey, Loretta E. Higgins, Josie L. Lascano, Ethel Fenton, Mrs. E. C. Hart, Mrs. Elsie L. Greilich, Edith Brown, Mrs. Myrtle Greer, Vivian E. Powers Marion E. Mellin, Mabel Moxness and Serena Karlhang, known to me to be the persons whose names are subscribed to the within instrument and acknowledged to me that they executed the same.

*[Signature: Arthur H. McCurdy]*
Notary Public in and for the County of Sacramento, State of California.

ARTHUR H. McCURDY
LAWYER
SACRAMENTO, CALIFORNIA

Articles of Incorporation for the Whisker Club of Camp '49 and the Whiskerette Club of Camp '49, Sacramento County Clerk Collection, Sacramento Archives & Museum Collection Center.

## *Bibliography*

Arthur H. McCurdy Collection [photographs], Sacramento Archives & Museum Collection Center, Sacramento, California.

Berger, Elinor, [photograph], Carson City, Nevada.

Best, Frank E., *Amidon Family: A Record of the Descendants of Roger Amadowne of Rehoboth, Mass.* (Chicago, IL: Frank Best, 1904).

British Pathe, *The End of the Chase* (1923), newsreel, http://www.britishpathe.com, Film ID 996.12 (accessed March 19, 2006).

City of Sacramento, "About the City of Sacramento," Feb. 6, 2006, www.cityofsacramento.org.

Cox, Joyce M., Head of Reference Services, Nevada State Library and Archives, Carson City, Nevada.

Davis, Winfield J., *An Illustrated History of Sacramento County, California: Containing a History of Sacramento County from the Earliest Period of Its Occupancy to the Present Time, Together with Glimpses of Its Prospective Future, Portraits of Some of Its Most Eminent Men, and Biographical Mention of Many of Its Pioneers and also Prominent Citizens of Today* (Chicago: Lewis Publishing Co., 1890).

Doherty, Augustus, newspaper articles, Nevada State Museum, Carson City, Nevada.

Getchell Library, University of Nevada, Reno, Nevada.

"Hans Langseth" [display], Catalog #387863, Research & Collections: Physical Anthropology Division, National Museum of Natural History, Smithsonian Institution, Washington, D.C.

Henley, James, in Dixie Reid, "Boom & Bust", Sacramento Bee, Dec. 31, 1999, www.sacbee.com

Jorgenson, Nils C., photographer, "Hans Langseth, King of the Whiskerinos" [photograph], Record #VM93-002978, Folio 13.1, Institute for Regional Studies, North Dakota State University, Fargo, North Dakota.

Massachusetts Office of the Secretary of State, *Massachusetts Soldiers and Sailors of the Revolutionary War: A Compilation from the Archives* (Boston, Wright and Potter Printing Co., State Printers, 1896).

"McKinney's Whiskerino Bear Hunt," Harry C. Peterson Papers, ca. 1880–1994, M0649, Department of Special Collections, Stanford University Libraries, Stanford University, Stanford, California.

Michael Benning Collection [photographs], Sacramento Archives & Museum Collection Center, Sacramento, California.

"Military Records of Zachary Wilcox, George Wilcox and John Faxon Wilcox," Compiled Military Service Files, National Archives and Records Administration, College Park, Maryland.

*Nevada Appeal*, Sept. 24, 1923–Jan. 3, 1927, Nevada State Library, Reno, Nevada.

"Nevada Census 1900," Nevada State Historical Preservation Office, State of Nevada Department of Cultural Affairs, Carson City, Nevada.

Nicodemus, Larry, photographs and genealogical records, private collection.

*Nevada Journal*, Aug. 3, 1915, Nevada State Library, Reno, Nevada.

"Pioneer of the West," photographs, Nevada Historical Society, Reno, Nevada.

Reid, Dixie, "Boom & Bust," *Sacramento Bee*, Dec. 31, 1999, www.sacbee.com.

*Reno Evening Gazette*, Jan. 1, 1927, Nevada State Library, Reno, Nevada.

Rickards, Herbert, Civil War Memorial Photos, private collection.

Riehl, Hattie, "Diary," private collection of Larry Nicodemus.

Riehl, Laurien E., photograph, and oral history, private collection.

Roe, Bruce, Whisker Club, Bremerton, Washington.

"Romance of California, The," 1922, Sacramento Room, Sacramento Public Library, Sacramento, California.

*Sacramento Bee,* March 2, 1922–Jan. 27, 1927; Sacramento Public Library, Sacramento, California.

Sacramento Photography Survey Collection, Sacramento Archives & Museum Collection Center, Sacramento, California.

Simpson, Meade, photographs, and oral history, private collection.

Stultz, David, Cemetery Sexton, Lone Mountain Cemetery.

Vaillant, Jeffrey, Sons of Union Veterans of the Civil War, personal communication with author.

"Vermont in the Civil War," Tom Ledoux, Aug. 23, 2005, http://www.vermontcivilwar.org.

Whiskerino and Whiskerette "Articles of Incorporation," Sacramento County Clerk Collection, Sacramento Archives & Museum Collection Center, Sacramento, California.

Will of Zachary Taylor Wilcox, Research and Reading Room, Nevada Historical Society, Reno, Nevada.

Witherell's Art & Antiques from the American West, "Presentation of Abe Lefton's Colt Single Action Revolver," (Accessed April 4, 2006)

*Index*

'49 Fete Rodeo, 19, 48, 49
Adams, Gwen L., 39, 99
Alaska Gold Rush, 16
Ambrose, C. A. "Ab," 19
Anapolsky, Bessie R., 99
Andrews, Lucia M., 99
Appomattox, 10. See also *Civil War.*
Archer, Alva S., 99
Archer, Nona, 38
Archer, Mrs. Martha, 38, 99
Articles of Incorporation, of the Whiskerinos and Whiskerettes, 24, 25, 83, 90–100
Barber's Union, 38
Bartine, Horace F., 13
Battle of Cedar Creek, 10. See also *Civil War.*
Beckstead, J., 13
Bell, Charles S., 50
Bellhouse, Mrs. Frank, 31
Bennett, C. C., 44
Benton's Stable, 20, 70
Berger, Elinor, 21
Bicycle, 21, 22
Bliss, Charles, 34
Board of Control, 59
Borres, J. J., Adjutant General, 33
Braslin, C. A., 13
British Pathe, 31, 66
Brown, Edith, 99
Burlingame, Jason C., 13
California, 7, 15, 18, 20, 24, 29, 30, 44, 50, 51, 55, 59, 68. See also *Sacramento* and *Chico.*
Califro, Miss Roe, 99
Callnon, John W., 93
Carson, Kit, 57
Carson City, 7, 10, 13, 16, 17, 20–22, 32, 55, 57–59, 61, 63, 69, 84
Chartz, John M., 7, 57
Chamber of Commerce. See *Sacramento.*
Chambers, 26. See also *McKinney's.*
Chariot races, 48
Charlottesville, occupation, 10. See also *Civil War.*
Chico, California, 15, 16, 33
Christian, Mrs. J. H., 99
Civil War, 2, 9, 15, 16, 58, 63, 64
Coloma, California, 68
Concord stagecoach, 20
Cooper, Mildred M., 90
C.P. Huntington No. 1, 52

Crawford, Flora, 99
Crown Prince, 6–8, 44, 45, 53, 66, 68
Custer, General George Armstrong, 10. See also *Civil War.*
*Daily Appeal* (Nevada), 58
Daly, J. S., 93
Davidson, Mrs. Ethel, 99
Days of '49 Celebration, 18, 19, 21, 22, 29, 38, 43, 45, 48, 49, 51, 53, 67, 67. See also *Sacramento* for costumes, mining town, planning, publicity, parade, password, rivalry, rodeo, song, whisker contest.
Delahaunty, Florence, 99
Dickerson, D.S., Governor, 13
Diggles, H. E., 23, 31, 34, 47, 57, 93
Dix, Hosea, 64
Dons of Peralta, 67
Dougherty, Augustus, 20
Dudley, Arthur, 23, 32
Dundas, Robert, 33
Dunn, Minnie, 99
Elliott, W. I. (Bill), 18, 19, 48, 49
*End of the Chase* (news broadcast), 66
Engler, Irvin, 23, 45, 47
Faustman, Bernice E., 92
Fenton, Ethel, 99
Fenton, Nell D., 99
First Congregational Church, 39
First Vermont Cavalry, 9, 10. See also *Civil War.*
Fitzgerald, Beulah, 99
Flu Epidemic, 17
Forest Ranch, California, 15
Funke, H. W., 93
G.A.R. See *Grand Army of the Republic.*
Galligher, Frank, 38
George V, King, 29, 30
Gilmore, Helen, 29
Gold Discovery Day, 55, 68
Gold rush, 16, 18, 30, 55
Gold Rush, Alaska. See *Alaska Gold Rush.*
Golden West, 3
Graham, Hazel, 99
Graham, William, 31
Grand Army of the Republic (G.A.R.), Custer Corps No. 15, Carson City, Nevada, 10, 12, 13, 58
Grand Lodge of Native Sons, 59
Grant, Ulysses S., 10
Greeley, Horace, 14, 20

Greer, Mrs. Myrtle, 99
Greilich, Mrs. Elsie L., 99
Gupton, C. C., 93
Handy, Ruth, 16. See also *Wilcox, Ruth.*
Harder, Hannah, 99
Hart, Mrs. E. C., 99
Hart, Elijah C., Judge, 23, 57, 67
Hawkins, Mae, 99
Henley, James, 17
Herspring, Madeline, 99
Herspring, Sheriff Joseph, 40, 47, 93
Hews, Nellie M., 99
Higgins, J. M., 57
Higgins, Loretta E., 99
Hosking, Teda, 99
Hughes, Charles Evans, 29
Independent Order of Odd Fellows, 58
Indian Camp, 20
Inman, J. M., State Senator, 68
Institute for Regional Studies, 47
International (news broadcast), 31
Iowa, 46, 65
Johnson, Fontaine, 34
Joyland Park, 67
Kangaroo Court, of the Whisker Club, 33
Karlhang, Serena, 99
Kensett, Iowa, 65
King, Gene B., 99
King of the Whiskerinos, 44, 45, 47, 65. See also *Langseth, Hans.*
Kinograms (news broadcast), 31
Kitzmeyer, G. E., 7, 57
Kitzmeyer, Oliver and Kenny, 58
Koening, Theodore N., 93
Kubel, Mrs. Annie, 99
Kuster, Mrs. A. J., 99
Kuster, Betty, 99
Langseth, Hans, 44, 45, 47, 65
LaRash, Jeff L., 34
Lascano, Josie L., 99
Last Will and Testament, of Zachary Wilcox. See *Will, of Zachary Wilcox.*
Lee, 10
Lefton, Abe, 49
Lewis, J. H., Senator, 29
Lewis, Ralph, 93
Lewis & Clark Expedition, 68
Lievre Girls, 27
Lodge, Henry Cabot, Senator, 29
Lone Mountain Cemetery, 63
Marshall, John, 68
Marysville, California 33
McCabe, Adellia McCurdy. See *McCurdy, Adellia.*

McCullough, John, 13
McCurdy, Adellia, 36, 38, 99
McCurdy, Arthur H., 7, 23, 36–40, 45, 47, 52, 93
McCurdy, Edith, 38, 99
McCurry, Harold J., 93
McKinney's, 26. See also *Chambers.*
Mellin, Marion E., 99
Membership cards, 28, 30
Mexican American War, 13, 20
Meyers, George, 13
Miner's Congress Parade, 38
Miner's Pot-Luck, 74
Mining Town, 19, 20, 29, 44, 49, 51
Minnesota, 46
Moreing Park, 32
Monk, Hank, 20
Moxness, Mabel, 99
National Archives and Records Administration, 11
National Museum of Natural History, 65, 66
Nevada, 7, 13, 15, 20, 41, 50, 63, 69, 89
*Nevada Daily Appeal.* See *Daily Appeal (Nevada).*
Nevada Historical Society, 41, 69, 70, 89
Nevada State Museum, 20
Nicodemus, Larry, 8, 12, 15, 21, 41
Nielsen, Sophie, 99
North Dakota, 44, 46
North Dakota State University. See *Institute for Regional Studies.*
Nunneley, D. G. "Dick," 31
Nunneley, Mrs. Emma, 99
Oakland, California, 40, 67
Ogden, Betty, 99
Oroville, California, 33
Pacific Coast League, 32
Palmer, Bertha R., 99
Parker, Dora, 99
Parkinson, V. E., 99
Parsons, Sarah. See *Wilcox, Sarah.*
Pathe News. See *British Pathe.*
Peterson, Harry, 23, 26, 68
Physical Anthropology Hall, 65, 66
Piute Tribe, 20
Polly, 22
*Pony Express* (film), 67
Posey, Eleanor H., 99
Powers, Vivian E., 99
Prohibition, 17
Reich Girls, 27
Reno, Nevada, 20
Revolutionary War Patriot, 15
Rickards, Herbert, 63, 64

Riehl, Laurien E., 13
Ringling Brothers Circus, 46
Robotham, Norman H., 93
Rodeo, 19, 48, 49
Roe, Bruce, 71
Romance of California, 18, 51
Russell, Cliff, 18, 73
Sacramento, 7, 17–20, 22, 23, 25, 27–40, 43–45, 47–53, 57–62, 65, 67–69, 72–74, 78–81; ball games, 32; brochure, 18, 19, 74–78; Chamber of Commerce, 23, 28, 32, 33, 48, 51, 74, 78; city charter, 18; costumes, 19, 27, 38, 71; contests, 6, 28, 29, 31, 43, 44, 49, 71; lapel buttons, 19, 31; mining town, 19, 20, 29, 44, 49, 51; parade, 19, 32, 37, 38, 43, 49, 58, 67; publicity, 18, 19, 28, 34, 40, 48, 67; rivalry, 48; rodeo, 19, 48, 49; song, 19, 79, 80; tourists, 18; Whiskers Court, 33
Sacramento Archives & Museum Collection Center, 2, 23, 25, 31, 35–40, 44, 45, 52, 65, 100
*Sacramento Bee*, 2, 28, 30, 32–35, 43, 44, 48, 50, 51, 53, 58–60, 81
Sacramento Junior College, 35
Sacramento Public Library, 2, 27, 37, 73, 74, 78, 79
*Sacramento Star*, 34
San Francisco, California, 20, 32, 40
Seavey, Clyde L., 23, 29–32, 34, 45, 47, 93
Selbnick News (news broadcast), 29
Shaving, 16, 31, 71
Sheridan's Raid, 10
Spencer Carbine, 10–11
Sierra Nevada Mountains, 15, 50
Silverman, Maurice, 19, 79, 80
Simpson, Edgar, 18, 19, 48
Simpson, Meade, 18, 28, 45, 48, 49
Smith, E. P., 31
Smith, M. D., 31
Smithsonian Institution, 65, 66
Snider, Mrs. Lillian, 38, 99
Sons of Union Veterans of the Civil War, 63. See also *Civil War*.
Southern Pacific Depot, 19, 33, 52, 58, 68
Spanish American War, 13
State Capitol, Sacramento, 32, 50, 58
Stanford University Libraries, 26, 68
Stephens, W.D., Governor, 32, 44
Stewart, Regina M., 99
Sutters Fort, 23, 50, 58, 59, 61
Swannell, W. L., 31
Taylor, Zachary, President, 33
Templeton, G. M., 31
Thirty-First Massachusetts Regiment, 9. See also *Civil War*.
Tucker, J. L., 57
Twain, Mark, 22
Tyner, George S., 19, 79, 80
University of Nevada, Reno, 2
Van Sandt, Mrs., 38
VanVoorhies Co., 47
Vermont, 8, 9, 10, 43, 64
Volcano, California, 20
Washoe Tribe, 20
Whisker Club, 3, 6, 22–24, 26, 28, 30, 32–35, 37, 39, 40, 43–45, 48, 49, 53, 57–59, 61, 62, 65, 67, 68, 71, 72, 83, 90–100
Whisker Club of Bremerton, 71
Whisker Contest. See *Sacramento*.
Whiskerette Club of Camp. '49. See *Whisker Club*.
Whiskerettes. See *Whisker Club*.
Whiskerinos. See *Whisker Club*.
Whiskerinos Club. See *Whisker Club*.
Whiskers Club of Camp '49. See *Whisker Club*.
Whiskers Club of Sacramento. See *Whisker Club*.
Whitingham, Vermont, 9, 64
Wilbur, Talma Zetta, 99
Wilcox, Andrew, 9, 15, 16, 64
Wilcox, Charles Luman, 9
Wilcox, Ella, 15, 16
Wilcox, Eliza, 15
Wilcox, Fiducia, 9, 64
Wilcox, George, 9, 10, 13, 15, 16, 64
Wilcox, John Faxon, 9, 10, 42, 64
Wilcox, Ruth, 16, 64. See also *Handy, Ruth*.
Wilcox, Sally, 9, 64
Wilcox, Sarah (Parsons), 9
Wilcox, Zachary Taylor, 7; accident, 22; beard, 16, 17, 20, 22, 32, 41–45, 47, 53, 55, 57–62, 69, 81; bicycle, 21, 22; Carson City, 16, 17; Chico, 15; death of and grave, 57–64; farmer, 7–9; military, 9–13; mining, 15, 16; mysterious end, 7, 57–62; news broadcasts, 66; photos, 8, 11–13, 21, 41, 44, 45, 47, 69, 70, 81; will of, 3, 7, 21, 41, 53, 55–61, 83–89
Wild West, 19
Will, of Zachary Wilcox, 3, 4, 7, 21, 41, 53–61, 83–89
Willard, Alexander H., 68
Winchester, Mr., 64
Women's Council, 29
Women's Relief Corps, 58
Women's Secret Service System, 39, 40

Women's Vigilance Committee, 39
World Beard and Moustache Association, 71
Work, George A., 93
Yukon, 16
Zimmerman, Anna, 99

Made in the USA
Lexington, KY
26 May 2011